Raoul Wallenberg

The Man Who Stopped Death

Raoul Wallenberg in 1935. (Courtesy of the Raoul Wallenberg Committee of the United States)

Raoul Wallenberg

The Man Who Stopped Death

SHARON LINNÉA

The Jewish Publication Society
Philadelphia and Jerusalem
5753 / 1993

The Jewish Publication Society, 1930 Chestnut Street,
Philadelphia, PA 19103.
Manufactured in the United States of America

Library of Congress Cataloging-in-Publication Data

Linnea, Sharon.
    Raoul Wallenberg : the man who stopped death / Sharon
Linnea.
        p. cm.
    Includes index.
    Summary: Traces the life of the Swedish diplomat who
saved Hungarian Jews during World War II and then
mysteriously disappeared after the Russians occupied
Budapest.
    ISBN 0–8276–0440–8 (cloth)
    ISBN 0–8276–0448–3 (pbk.)
    1. Jews—Hungary—Persecutions—Juvenile literature.
    2. Wallenberg, Raoul—Juvenile literature.   3. Righteous
Gentiles in the Holocaust—Biography—Juvenile
literature.   4. Diplomats—Sweden—Biography—Juvenile
literature.   5. World War, 1939–1945—Jews—Rescue—
Hungary—Juvenile literature.   6. Holocaust, Jewish
(1939–1945)—Hungary—Juvenile literature.   7. Hungary—
Ethnic relations—Juvenile literature.   8. Sweden—
Biography—Juvenile literature. [1. Wallenberg, Raoul.   2.
Diplomats.   3. World War, 1939–1945—Jews—Rescue.   4.
Holocaust, Jewish (1939–1945)—Hungary.] I. Title.
DS135.H9L53   1993
940.54′77943912′092—dc20
[B]   93–12140
                                                          CIP
                                                          AC

Designed by Joanna Hill
Typeset in Trump Medieval text and
    Gills Sans display by Ruttle, Shaw & Wetherill
Printed by Haddon Craftsmen

10 9 8 7 6 5 4 3

FOR RAOUL
and to the memory of
Leslie Howard,
born Laszlo Stainer,
the son of Hungarian Jews,
in the fervent hope
that art will continue to inspire action

Contents

CONTENTS

Author's Note

This is a true story. The people named in this narrative are actual people, and the thrust of each conversation reported here has been documented. There are three exceptions. The taxi driver in Chapter 10, "Susanna" in Chapter 13, and "Hannah" in Chapter 19 are composite characters blending together several "real life" people.

Acknowledgments

Heartfelt thanks to those who were there and who continue to share so much of themselves so that the story of those times will never be forgotten. My special gratitude goes to Elizabeth Kasser, Baroness Elisabeth Kemeny-Fuchs, Tom and Annette Lantos, Viveca Lindfors, and Tom Veres, not all of whom appear by name in the text, but all of whom gave freely of their personal reminiscences and thereby shaped the story. Thanks also to Rachel Oestreicher Haspel, president of the Raoul Wallenberg Committee of the United States, who first suggested this project and who provided "The Legend of the Just," which opens her own talks; and to the Raoul Wallenberg Committee of the United States for unlimited use of archival materials, as well as rare books, journals, and letters.

Finally, thanks to Robert Owens Scott, who made this book happen.

Raoul Wallenberg

The Man Who Stopped Death

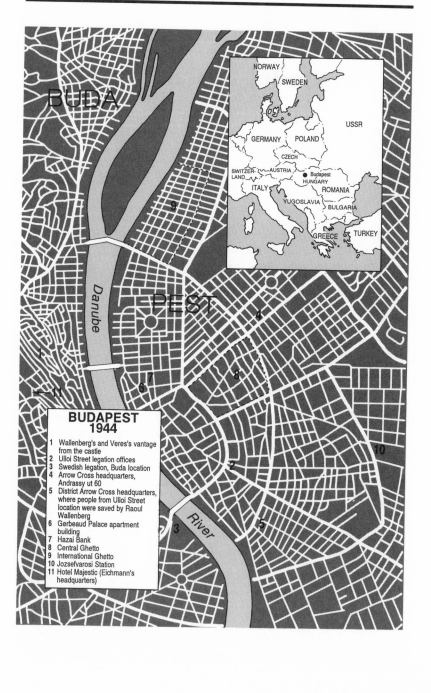

**BUDAPEST
1944**

1 Wallenberg's and Veres's vantage
   from the castle
2 Ulloi Street legation offices
3 Swedish legation, Buda location
4 Arrow Cross headquarters,
   Andrassy ut 60
5 District Arrow Cross headquarters,
   where people from Ulloi Street
   location were saved by Raoul
   Wallenberg
6 Gerbeaud Palace apartment
   building
7 Hazai Bank
8 Central Ghetto
9 International Ghetto
10 Jozsefvarosi Station
11 Hotel Majestic (Eichmann's
   headquarters)

I.

The Legend of the Just

The Jewish people have a legend. It says there must be thirty-six truly good people alive at all times if the world is to go on. These are people of quiet courage. They come forward at times of great danger and use their powers to defeat evil. When the battle is over, they disappear.

Many think that such a hero appeared in this century in the darkest days of World War II, at the same time that a Nazi named Adolph Eichmann came to the city of Budapest in Hungary. Eichmann knew the Nazis were losing the war, but he wasn't ready to give up. It was his job to kill all the Jewish people in Europe, and he had done this job very well. Millions of men, women, and children were already murdered. The only large group of Jews left alive were in Budapest.

Everyone in town knew when Colonel Eichmann came and why. The old men closed up their shops. The young mothers snatched their children off the streets and stayed inside. The teenagers stopped meeting at movies and cafés. At dusk, as night came, often a boy or girl would slip out of a dark house and go to a friendly neighbor to get some milk or bread. Then he or she would slip home through patrolled streets. If they were caught, they would be killed at once. What had they done wrong? Nothing. But their mother or father was Jewish.

They knew Mr. Eichmann planned to kill them all.

Who could help? The Americans and the British were too far away. The Soviet army was coming, but it made slow progress. The men in town who were ambassadors from other countries were badly outnumbered. Eichmann's men had guns and would shoot anyone who tried to stop them.

Just when there was no hope, one man appeared.

He was a young man with brown hair. He wore a jacket and carried a backpack. He told Adolph Eichmann, "You cannot kill these people."

"Who will stop me?" sneered the Nazi.

"I will," he said.

Eichmann was amazed at this man's foolish courage. The colonel knew one man alone couldn't possibly stop battalions of Nazis.

But Adolph Eichmann didn't know Raoul Wallenberg.

2.

The Story of Two Raouls

Thirty years before this terrible time, a handsome young man stood on the deck of the Royal Navy ship, the *Gota*. Darkness came early in Sweden in the early months of the year, and he turned up the collar of his thick gray officer's coat to keep out the chilly wind. It was March 18, 1910. Behind him, the sailors who weren't on duty greeted and joked with each other. They were excited to be sailing the next day. But Raoul stood, not looking toward the sea, but looking toward his home city of Stockholm. It was clear he was thinking about something else.

Finally he made up his mind. He pushed his hands into his pockets and strode down the gangplank. In the guardhouse he cranked the phone. He told the operator he wished to ring Dr. Wising's house. As he hoped, the telephone was answered by Dr. Wising's youngest daughter.

"Maj, this is Raoul Wallenberg," he said. "I know I called on you last night to say good-bye before I sailed. But I'd like to visit again. Now."

"Raoul," she said, "is anything wrong?"

"Please ask your parents if I may come."

In a minute she was back. "Of course you may."

As Raoul rode the streetcar through the well-lit streets of Stockholm, he almost laughed at himself. The life of a sailor never frightened him. Neither did the fierce wind or the briny waves during terrible storms at sea. How could he be afraid to talk to a girl?

Raoul jumped off the streetcar and walked to the Wising's street. His breath came out in little puffs of frosty air. He paused only a moment in front of her house before he opened the garden gate.

Beautiful Maj was waiting for him. She came down the walk to invite him inside, but he took her hand. "Stay out here with me for a minute," he said. He took off his heavy coat and put it around her slight shoulders.

"Maj, I can't hope that you care for me very much," he said.

She looked up at him, surprised. Then she laughed. "Raoul, for weeks I have been in a huff because I didn't think you cared about me at all!"

When her blue eyes danced that way, it was hard for him to speak. "Why—I love you, Maj Wising, and I can do nothing but ask you to marry me!"

"If you put it that way, Mr. Wallenberg," she replied, "I can do nothing but accept!"

When they finally went inside, the night no longer seemed cold, and the stars seemed to Raoul to be as close as the sparkle in Maj's eyes.

Raoul and Maj's wedding was one of the happiest in Stockholm. The Wallenberg family was well known in Sweden, and the Wisings had many friends as well. The party at the Grand Hotel went on for hours.

After the wedding, Raoul's father and mother sailed back to Japan, where his father was the Swedish ambassador. Raoul was their only child, and they wished the young couple well.

Several months later, Maj and Raoul found out they were expecting a baby. This made them happier than ever. But their joy was not to last.

Raoul became ill very suddenly. The pain in his stomach became worse and worse. The best doctors in Sweden were called in to see him.

"We're very sorry, Mrs. Wallenberg," the head doctor said, "but your husband has cancer."

"Isn't there anything you can do?" Maj pleaded.

The doctor shook his head sadly. "I've never seen a disease spread so fast."

As the months went by, Raoul became weaker and weaker. Soon he couldn't even get out of bed. Maj could see the terrible pain in his eyes, but he never complained.

One day at the beginning of summer, she came to sit by his bed. Outside, the air was warm and children played kick-ball in the gardens. Raoul took his wife's hand. He smiled at her. "Today you turn twenty-one years old. Happy birthday, my little Maj! I'm sorry I don't have a gift for you."

Maj put his hand against her cheek. "All I want is for you to get well. You must get well!"

"If I could live, I would," he whispered. "For you, Maj, and for our child. But I know I'm going to die." He felt her warm tears on his cold hand. He took his other hand and put it on her round belly. "I would be so happy if only little Baby grows into a kind and good human being."

"I'll do my best," Maj answered. "That will be my gift to you."

A few days later, Raoul died. He was buried in his best military clothes. After everyone left, Maj put his shiny sword on top of his grave.

She went to stay with her parents. They had a summer

house on a beautiful island not far from Stockholm. When Maj was growing up, she loved to stay there. She walked among the birch trees and breathed the salty air. Now she felt nothing but sadness. Often she sat by the window for hours without saying a word.

"What are you thinking, Maj?" her mother asked.

"Sometimes I miss Raoul so badly that I wish I had died, too," she said.

Mrs. Wising knew it wouldn't help to tell her daughter not to be sad. Only time could bring back Maj's happiness.

"You have a child to think of now," she said softly.

"I will be strong for Baby," Maj said, "but it must know its mother has a broken heart."

On Saturday afternoon, August third, the midwife Miss Cedarholm called Dr. Bovin to come to the Wisings' house. Maj's child was on the way. Mrs. Wising and the doctor and nurse stayed with Maj all evening. The doctor asked if she wanted some chloroform, but Maj wanted to be awake to see her child.

On August 4, 1912, in the summer light of Sunday's early hours, the baby was born. "He's beautiful, Mrs. Wallenberg, a fine boy!" said Dr. Bovin.

"He's got a caul on his head. That means he's marked for greatness," Miss Cedarholm said as she washed the small fellow and wrapped him in a blanket.

As they handed the baby to Maj, he struggled to open his brown eyes for the first time. As she looked at him, it seemed to her that she saw all the happiness and love that she thought were lost to her forever.

Maj looked at her mother and smiled. "We'll call him Raoul," she said.

3.

The "Big Men"

Young Raoul grew quickly. As much as he loved the outdoor life on the small island, there were so many interesting things to explore back in the city!

One day when Raoul was four, Maj met an old friend on one of the streets of downtown Stockholm. After they had chatted for a while, she looked down to take Raoul's hand but he had disappeared.

The two women called him until Maj's friend suddenly said, "Maj! Over there!"

Young Raoul had gone to a construction site where a new building was going up. He stood between the architect and the engineer seriously studying the building blueprint with the men. Maj saw him pointing and asking questions.

"I'm so sorry!" she said as she grabbed his hand.

"Don't worry, ma'am," said the architect. "I wish our workers asked as many questions as this little fellow!"

When Raoul was six years old, his mother married a health department official named Frederik von Dardel. Mr. von Dardel was a kind man who treated Raoul like his very own. Soon Raoul had a sister named Nina and a little brother named Guy.

But Raoul never forgot that he was a Wallenberg.

Grandfather Gustav Wallenberg was now Sweden's ambassador to the mysterious country of Turkey. Whenever his grandparents came home to Sweden, they sent for Raoul at once.

Grandfather Wallenberg (or Farfar, as Swedish children call their father's father) told Raoul exciting stories about the Wallenbergs in days gone by. Jacob Wallenberg had been a sea captain back in the 1760s, when it was very dangerous to cross the stormy oceans. Jacob helped open trade routes to the faraway lands of China and Japan. He also wrote rousing adventure books about his voyages.

Raoul's great-grandfather, Andre Oscar, went to sea when he was fifteen. He was still a young man when he became captain of a steamer. He was elected to Sweden's congress, called the Riksdag, and he opened the Enskilda Bank, which helped start many Swedish companies. Andre Oscar had twenty children. His sons became diplomats and bankers. Farfar was one of his sons.

Raoul loved to listen to the stories Farfar told about his own life in faraway China and Japan and now in Turkey. He secretly dreamed of being one of the "Big Men," like the Wallenbergs of old. They seemed like fearless Vikings to him, sailing off on adventures and returning in glory.

And then, during one of their visits, Farfar told Raoul his own secret dream. He wanted to open up a world bank that would serve not only Sweden, but the whole world. Farfar had planned to start this bank with his own son. "It's a great loss to both of us that your father is dead," Farfar said. "Perhaps, if you have the talent for it, I'll open the bank with you."

Raoul blushed with pride. He had never been very interested in banking, but it would be a great honor to do something so important with his grandfather.

"I'll work very hard, Grandfather," he said.

"If it's to be a world bank, you must know about the world," Farfar said. "Study languages, and read the newspapers, young Raoul, and we'll see what will happen. We'll see."

Raoul's father, Raoul Wallenberg, in navy uniform. (Courtesy of the Raoul Wallenberg Committee of the United States)

Raoul's mother, Maj Wising, in 1911. (Courtesy of the Raoul Wallenberg Committee of the United States)

Raoul with his grandfather, Gustav Wallenberg (Far-far). (Courtesy of the Raoul Wallenberg Committee of the United States)

4.

Finding Adventures

Raoul might not have been very interested in banking, but he was curious about how people lived in other countries. During Raoul's summer vacations, Farfar took him to visit friends in England, Germany, and France. Back home, Raoul studied English, French, and German so that he could talk to his new friends in their own languages.

When Raoul was twelve years old, Farfar sent him a ticket to go by boat and train from Stockholm all the way to Istanbul, Turkey. It was a test. Farfar wanted Raoul to think he was all on his own. Then he quietly paid the train conductor to keep a sharp eye on the boy.

The most interesting part of the journey came unexpectedly in Yugoslavia. As the train arrived in the capital city of Belgrade, it was surrounded by a noisy mob staging a political demonstration. Curious, Raoul called, "What's going on? What are you demonstrating about?"

The crowd was too busy to answer a boy hollering on a train.

A few minutes later, the conductor stopped by Raoul's compartment. The boy was nowhere to be seen.

"Where is he?" he asked the other passengers.

Raoul at twelve in 1924. (Courtesy of the Raoul Wallenberg Committee of the United States)

In response, one man pointed outside to the mass of people.

An hour later the whistle blew signaling that the train was ready to leave the station. The conductor had looked everywhere without success. What would he tell Ambassador Wallenberg?

As the engine picked up speed, the passengers saw a tall boy racing for the train. Raoul barely caught it and got a foothold on the moving steps. Gasping for breath, he collapsed into his seat, his backpack on his back.

"Interesting town," he said happily.

In Istanbul, Raoul sat nervously as the conductor told Farfar of Raoul's actions. At the end of the story, Farfar stood up. "Thank you for your help, sir," he said. "I'll take care of the boy myself."

After the conductor left, Farfar closed the door to his study. He sat down and looked at his grandson. Finally, he could no longer hide his smile. "Well, what was the demonstration about?" Farfar boomed. "I hope you learned something useful!"

One of the best public schools in Stockholm was called the New Elementary School. Raoul went there from the time he was nine until he graduated from high school at seventeen. He had a smart and fun-loving group of friends, boys who were as curious about the world as he was and enjoyed a good time. One thing he especially liked was debate. He told his sister, Nina, that he loved to get people to agree with his ideas without letting them know he was doing it.

But, most of all, he loved to draw. Raoul drew landscapes, people, pictures of anything. Whenever there was a school dance or party, his schoolmates asked Raoul to make a special poster.

Although Raoul went to all the school dances, he still hadn't learned to dance. Nina knew he was shy around girls.

"Did you have fun tonight?" she asked him one night after a high school dance.

"Yes," Raoul answered, smiling at her because he knew she was teasing him. "As a matter of fact, I met a very smart girl. We talked all night."

"Oh, yes? What did she have to say?"

"Actually, I told her about the League of Nations. Sweden must find its place—"

"I see," Nina cut him off with a sigh. "It seems a smart girl is one who knows how to listen!"

5.

Getting Ready

Raoul was excited about going to college at the University of Michigan in the United States. Ann Arbor, Michigan, was a small town, but it would have a lot to teach him about American ways. Farfar agreed to let him study architecture, which he knew Raoul loved. He would learn about banking after college.

No one in Michigan had heard of the important Wallenberg family. Raoul was able to act like an ordinary student. He enjoyed eating hot dogs, wearing sneakers, and going to Laurel and Hardy movies on weekends. He covered his walls with brown packing paper and painted his bedroom to look like a green jungle with wild animals peeking through the leaves. He made friends quickly and went to many parties and concerts.

The only thing Raoul wasn't very good at was math. This wasn't a good sign for someone who was going to be a banker! Instead he worked hard drawing houses and buildings.

One day, the art teacher, Professor Jean Paul Slusser, called Raoul aside. "I think you could have a great career as a painter," he said.

Raoul tried to picture Farfar's face if he told him he

wasn't going to be a banker but a painter instead. It was all he could do to keep from laughing.

"Thank you very much, Professor," he said, "but I am expected to go into the family business."

During school vacations, Raoul traveled all around the country. He wanted to see as much of the United States as possible. He had an aunt back east in Connecticut and another down south in Mexico. His young cousins loved seeing him. He could draw anything, and he could make any animal sound they asked for.

He also traveled west to San Francisco. During the year of the presidential election, he went to Washington, D.C., to see how the U.S. government worked. He liked the United States very much.

Raoul hitchhiked everywhere. It wasn't safe, even back then, but it was a good way to meet lots of different people. During the summer of 1933, the World's Fair was in Chicago. Raoul worked there for the Swedish Exhibition, doing odd jobs for three dollars a day. When it came time for school to start again, he packed up and set out for Michigan.

At first it seemed Raoul was in luck. A gentleman in a fine car stopped and offered him a ride. The man was nice, but he talked very fast and drove even faster. They were going seventy miles per hour when they saw a train crossing the road in front of them. It was too late to slow down. The driver hit the brakes. The car went into a wild skid and slammed into the crossing sign.

"You all right, son?" the man asked when he found his voice.

"It seems that way," Raoul answered. They both climbed out and looked at the car. It was practically demolished.

"Close call," said the man. Raoul waited with him until

a tow truck came. He waved good-bye, then started along the side of the highway with his two suitcases. It was harder to hitchhike on the highway, but he had no other choice.

No one stopped. A warm August dusk painted the sky. Crickets chirped in the fields along the road. It would soon be dark, and Raoul was miles from the nearest town.

He was tired and hungry and beginning to worry when a Chevrolet with Iowa plates pulled over. Four men were inside. None of them looked very nice. But Raoul decided he had no other choice. He got in.

The young man who was driving was thin and unshaven. "Where ya goin'?" he asked.

"Back to school in Ann Arbor," Raoul said.

The man looked at Raoul's expensive leather suitcases. "How much is it worth to you to take you all the way to Ann Arbor?" he asked.

"Nothing," said Raoul, sensing he might be in for trouble. "If I had any money, I would have taken the bus. It's hard for foreign students to get work."

They rode in silence for a few miles. Then, suddenly, the driver swerved off the highway onto a small dirt road that ran into the woods. The car screeched to a stop.

"All right. Get out of the car," the driver said. Now his voice sounded like a growl. It was hard to see much in the darkness of the woods, but Raoul could see one thing: the driver had a gun.

He got out, and the four men surrounded him. "Give us your money," the leader said. Raoul took out his wallet and handed them the bills. The gun was still pointed at his head. He felt strangely calm, but he could see that the gunman was very nervous. So Raoul opened his suitcase and gave them his whole summer's savings.

17

"That's all I have, fellows," he said. "Now the least you can do is give me a ride back to the highway.

They hadn't expected such a request. "Get in the front seat," the driver growled. They put his heavy suitcase on his lap so that he couldn't do anything tricky. Without speaking to each other, the thieves drove back toward the road. Raoul's calmness made them more and more nervous. Finally, the driver leaned over to open Raoul's door. The men in the backseat pushed him out into a deep ditch. They threw his bags out on top of him.

Raoul stayed under his suitcases in case they decided to shoot him. They drove away instead.

By now it was night. His chance of finding another ride was slim. He decided to sleep in the ditch. He lay there thinking about what had just happened and what he might have done differently. He was glad he had stayed so calm in a dangerous situation. He wondered if he'd ever face such danger again. Eventually he drifted off to sleep.

Early the next morning, Raoul hiked through the woods to the train tracks. When a train came, he flagged it down. The thieves had never checked his pockets. He had just enough money left for a ticket to Ann Arbor.

Raoul finished his architectural degree in three and a half years, a year earlier than most of his classmates. He was eager to start on his future. As he sailed home to Sweden, he was looking forward to becoming partners with Grandfather Wallenberg in their new world bank.

Young Raoul stood by the rail of the ship, watching the ship slice through the mighty ocean waves. That's how he would face the future, he thought, head on! It seemed nothing could go wrong.

6.

The Seeds Are Sown

It was almost dark but the Haifa seaport in Palestine was still bustling. British sailors laughed and joked with each other while dock workers unloaded a newly docked cargo ship.

It was the fall of 1936, and Raoul was a year out of college. Usually, he noticed everything going on around him, but not tonight. He was on his way home from the post office, where he'd mailed a letter to Farfar. It was a hard letter to write, but Raoul knew he finally had to tell him the truth.

Raoul paused, looking over the water, thinking about his hectic year. From the United States, he had sailed home to Stockholm. There he had entered a design contest. Sweden's best architects had all entered and young Raoul won second place!

He hadn't been home long, though, before Farfar expected him to learn banking so that they could start their bank. But Farfar's plans weren't what Raoul expected. First, Farfar sent Raoul to Africa to work as a salesman for a chemical company. Raoul did his best, but he hated it. Next, Farfar sent Raoul to Palestine to work for a Dutch bank. He didn't like this job any better. Raoul knew he had to face the truth: he wasn't cut out to be a banker.

Raoul looked again at the small waves lapping against the boats in the harbor. He sighed. That was what he had written in his letter to Farfar. He had admitted that he didn't want to open a world bank. But this is what they had planned all these years. What would Farfar think? Would he even listen?

Laughter from a seaside restaurant floated past him, and Raoul knew he had to hurry home if he didn't want to miss dinner.

The long table was crowded at the rooming house where he was staying. The house was run by devout Jews who "kept kosher." They used one set of dishes for meat and another set for dairy. Thousands of Jewish people were coming to Palestine. Rooms were hard to find. There was almost always another boarder sharing Raoul's small room.

Sure enough, a friendly young man with a suitcase and valise was there that night.

"Hello!" the man said in German. He was surprised and happy when Raoul answered him in his own language. "Are you from Germany?" the young man asked.

"No," Raoul answered, "but I've visited often with my grandparents." The young man's valise was open. Raoul saw the corner of drawing paper. "Are you an architect?" he asked.

"Yes," answered his new friend. "My name is Ariel."

"I'm an architect, too!" Raoul said happily. "Can I take a look at your drawings?"

For almost an hour, the two young men pored over each other's designs. They had a lot in common. Finally, Raoul asked Ariel why he had left Berlin.

Ariel was suddenly silent. It was almost as if a dark cloud settled on his face. "Surely you've heard about the

Nuremberg Laws," he said. "About what they are doing to the Jewish people. All of our rights have been taken away. We can't find jobs. Our children aren't allowed to go to school. Our synagogues are being destroyed. Even our homes aren't safe anymore."

"Surely your friends and neighbors stand up for you?"

Ariel shook his head. "How can they? Hitler is claiming that Jews are traitors to Germany. Anyone who stands up for us is a traitor, too. But why? We're doctors, grocers, booksellers like everybody else. Many of us fought and died for Germany in the last war. But because of the Nazis, many Germans now hate us. It's dangerous for friends to help. I was lucky to get out with my suitcase and valise. Soon there will be no escape. I tremble to think what will happen!"

"I can't believe that propaganda and hatred will win," the Swede answered. "Good men and women will soon stand up and fight back."

"Where are these good men?" Ariel asked quietly. "I didn't see them when I ran for my life."

That night, Raoul lay awake for a long time thinking about what Ariel had said. It made him burn with anger. Just before he went to sleep, a different thought came to him. He hadn't felt so strongly about anything for a long time. At the bank all he did was count bills and tell people they couldn't borrow money.

"I don't want to spend my life telling people what they can't do," he thought. "I want to show people what they can do."

But his future was in Farfar's hands.

Or so he thought.

When Raoul finished his job at the bank in Haifa, he

went to see his grandparents in the south of France. Farfar looked old and tired, but he was still planning Raoul's future in banking. Farfar didn't even seem to remember Raoul's letter.

Raoul left his grandparents to visit his family in Stockholm. He was there in March 1937 when word came: Farfar was dead. Many people mourned Farfar's death, but perhaps it was hardest for Raoul. All his life he'd worked so hard to please the old man. All his life he'd tried to fulfill his grandfather's dreams. Now what would he do?

7.

The Hard Years

The next years were hard ones. Raoul wasn't allowed to work as an architect in Sweden because his degree was from an American university. The whole world was in a very bad economic depression. Jobs were hard to find. There wasn't even a place for Raoul at the Enskilda Bank, which was run by his uncles. Raoul started some businesses of his own. But as hard as he worked, the companies failed.

By 1939, Nazi leader Adolph Hitler had become the dictator of Germany. Hitler had put thousands of unemployed Germans to work building guns, tanks, and weapons. He organized members of his Nazi party into an army. He then started to make alliances with or take over the countries near Germany, including Austria, Poland, and France. Hitler's Nazis believed that he would save Germany and give them work. The German people, Hitler said, were members of a master race destined to rule the world.

Sweden was known for remaining neutral in wartime. Its leaders thought it best to stay out of wars that were being fought between other countries. This position was hard for Raoul to accept from the very beginning. If a great wrong was being done, he felt that it was important to fight it, even if it didn't affect him directly. Raoul began to work quietly to help Jewish people who'd fled to Sweden to escape the Nazis.

He eventually got a job working for a man named Kalman Lauer, who exported specialty foods from Sweden to Hungary and other European countries. He was Jewish and could no longer travel freely. Raoul was educated, was an excellent bargainer, and could speak German, French, and English fluently. He soon became a junior partner in Kalman Lauer's firm.

In Sweden in those days, young men and women enjoyed dances on Saturday nights. Usually the dances were held at friends' homes. Sometimes they were very formal, with an orchestra, and everyone would dress up in suits and long dresses. But most of the time the host provided sandwiches and pastries, and the guests danced to the latest records played on the phonograph. They'd do the waltz, the tango, or the foxtrot.

One Saturday night, Raoul was introduced to the cousin of his friend who was hosting the dance. The cousin's name was Viveca Lindfors. She was to become a popular actress in both Sweden and the United States. At the time she was a pretty young woman of seventeen or eighteen studying to become an actress. Although she was much younger than Raoul, he enjoyed her vitality. The second time he met her, he asked her if she'd like to go out to the movies one night. Raoul wasn't as handsome as many of the boys Viveca dated. But he was nice enough, so she accepted the intense young man's invitation.

After the movie, Raoul invited Viveca back to his apartment, which had once belonged to his grandfather. At the time, most girls wore colors such as navy blue. Viveca, however, was wearing a black dress and black stockings. It made her feel very sophisticated and very dramatic. Raoul opened a door off the hallway and invited her in. "This was my grandfather's office," he said.

Viveca looked around. The furniture was made of wood or leather, and the dark, rich colors made the room seem warm. Raoul closed the doors, and they sat down. He leaned forward and started to whisper. Viveca leaned forward to hear what he was saying. "Terrible things are happening, Viveca, to the Jews in Germany and the countries Hitler is taking over. He says he's 'resettling' people, but he's not. They're being killed. By the thousands. The millions, soon, if no one stops him."

The girl was stunned—not at the news he was whispering, but that anyone on a date would talk about something as distasteful as politics, or what was happening to strange people in a faraway land. Was he trying to impress her with his travels and his knowledge?

"Even the Jewish people don't really believe it. But they haven't seen the camps in France where people are treated like dogs. Or heard about piles of bodies left to rot in the woods of Poland. Old women and small children who couldn't do Hitler any harm. Dead out of hatred and no other reason."

Viveca studied Raoul's face as he talked. She'd never seen anyone quite so intense. Was he telling her these things to gain her sympathy? If so, it wasn't working. For one thing, she didn't believe any of it. Many Swedes were impressed by what the Nazi party said here in Sweden. But the Nazis certainly didn't say anything about murdering children or anybody else. It was unbelievable!

25

"Don't you see?" he was finishing. "If something isn't done soon, it will be too late!"

"Yes, sure," she said politely. "Thanks for a wonderful evening. I really must get home."

As Raoul helped her on with her coat, she was still trying to pinpoint what made him so different. He'd traveled a lot, for one thing. Perhaps he knew too much. He wasn't silly and fun like the others in her crowd. One thing was sure. This was the least romantic date she'd ever had.

Later, when Viveca Lindfors found out what Raoul said was true, she wished she could go back and have the kind of deep conversation Raoul wanted to have. She wished she and her Swedish friends—and most of the world—had been willing to listen to what Raoul and others like him were trying to say.

Raoul's job took him through many countries that were torn by war. Often he visited Mr. Lauer's native country of Hungary. Whenever possible, he looked up Mr. Lauer's relatives.

Hungary was in a special situation. Since Admiral Horthy, the leader of Hungary, had made a pact with Hitler, Germany left Hungary alone. In the capital city of Budapest, people could almost pretend there was no war. The cafés were still open on the banks of the Danube River. People still worked and went to school and had parties.

Raoul knew the Lauer family was Jewish. The Hungarian Jews had heard stories about what was happening. But the stories were very hard to believe, especially when no one wanted to believe them. They'd heard about the massacre of Jewish people near them in Yugoslavia. But many of the Jews in Hungary were well educated and well off.

They didn't believe anything would happen to them. Besides, even if they did know, what could they do? What could anyone do?

One snowy winter evening in February of 1942, Raoul's sister Nina had a "date" with her older brother. He had just returned from a business trip to Hungary, Switzerland, and Germany, and she was very interested in the news he would bring. When Raoul was in Stockholm, he often stopped by his old home for breakfast or dinner to visit the family. Tonight he and Nina were invited to the British embassy to see a new movie starring the dashing English actor Leslie Howard.

The film was called *Pimpernel Smith*. Leslie Howard had starred in an earlier movie called *The Scarlet Pimpernel*. In that film he played a rich man in long-ago France who pretended to be spoiled and silly. But secretly at night he saved people from death at the hands of the government.

Pimpernel Smith was a modern version of the story. In this new movie, Leslie Howard played a seemingly boring professor who secretly saved many Jewish people from the Nazis. As Nina watched the film, she had to smile because the tall, elegant Howard looked very much like Raoul!

As they left the embassy, heading home through the snowy night, Nina thought Raoul was quieter than usual. "Did you like the movie?" she asked.

Raoul put a brotherly arm around her shoulder. His response was unexpected: "I want to do exactly what he did."

In early 1944, in the midst of a world torn by war and hardship, a most unlikely thing happened. Raoul

27

fell in love with a beautiful woman named Jeanette. Jeanette was as upset as Raoul about the war. Smart and a good listener, she could find something to laugh about even in the darkest times.

One spring day Raoul, happy himself, went with Jeanette to Drottningholm, a park surrounding a beautiful castle outside of Stockholm. They held hands and talked and laughed. Then they went to a romantic outdoor café and ordered coffee. Suddenly, Raoul took Jeanette's hand and said, "I would very much like you to marry me."

Jeanette was very surprised. "Oh, Raoul," she said. "I'm very flattered. I like you very much, but I'm not even twenty years old. I'm too young to think about getting married!"

She tried to make light of it, Raoul knew. But the fact was that he had asked her to marry him, and she had refused. It seemed very little was going right in his life.

He had no idea that within days his whole life would change forever.

8.

Opportunity Knocks

On June 9, 1944, Raoul's partner, Kalman Lauer, asked him to come to dinner at an expensive restaurant outside of Stockholm. He wanted Raoul to meet Ivar Olsen from the War Refugee Board in the United States.

Mr. Olsen came right to the point. "We've found out that the Jews in Budapest are in terrible danger," he said.

Raoul and Mr. Lauer did not look at each other. "Yes, I know," said Raoul.

Mr. Lauer had written urgent letters to his wife's family in Hungary and had received no answer.

"The reports we've gotten about Adolph Hitler's 'Final Solution' are unbelievable," said Mr. Olsen.

"The Nazis have already killed millions of people—old people, women, and little children," Raoul said.

"Anyone who has any Jewish blood," finished the American. "They've been stuffed onto trains like herds of cattle and taken to camps. Then they're made to go into large rooms." He could not finish.

"I know," Raoul said quietly. "They're killed with gas."

"The only large group of Jews left alive in Europe are in Hungary," Mr. Olsen continued. "We've got to save them. Hitler won't let an American into Hungary, of course. The country still has its own leader, but it's under Hitler's control. We need someone from a neutral country to go to save the Jews. We hear that you speak German and that you know your way around Budapest. We also hear you're good at bargaining with people. Do you think you could bargain for lives? Think hard before you answer. It will be dangerous if you go."

"There isn't time to think hard," Raoul said. "If we want to save anyone, I have to leave right now."

"Wallenberg, you're not even Jewish. How can the Swedish rabbis know you're serious?" asked Mr. Olsen.

"When innocent people are being murdered, we're all fellow human beings."

"You seem to have everything we need for the job," said Mr. Olsen. "I'll tell our committee about you."

"First let me tell you what I need," said Raoul.

The men looked at him in surprise.

"There is no time left to play by the rules," said Raoul. "If I go to Budapest, I must be free to do whatever I can to save lives. I won't have time to write out reports or answer to a boss. I must be allowed to come and go as I please. I must be able to talk to the ruler of Hungary and the rabbis and Mr. Eichmann. I must also have a lot of money." He smiled. "Often those who won't listen when people talk will listen to money."

"I'll report this to the committee," said Mr. Olsen.

"Please report it fast," said Raoul. "Or there will be no one left to save."

Mr. Olsen knew immediately Raoul was the man for the job. The Jewish leaders, the king of Sweden, and the Americans all gave their approval. He was given the passport and title of a Swedish diplomat. But his money and his mission secretly came from the United States. He knew he'd be killed if the Germans ever found out he was working for their enemies, the Americans.

9.

Train to Budapest

To take a train to Budapest, Raoul had to fly to Berlin, the Nazi capital. His sister, Nina, met him there on the afternoon of July 2, 1944. She was living there with her husband, Gunnar, who was also working as a diplomat. Nina was expecting her first baby, and she was glad for the chance to see her brother.

"We've gotten you a train ticket for Saturday," Nina said. "We'll give you a good dinner and hear all the news from home."

"Thanks for buying me a ticket," he said, "but I can't wait until Saturday. Not even a day can be spared. I must leave tomorrow!"

"But it's impossible to get you a first-class seat so soon. It may be impossible to get you any seat at all!"

"I must go at once," Raoul said. "More lives are lost every day."

Nina knew this tone in her brother's voice. When he'd made up his mind, it was no use trying to change it.

That night, air raid sirens split the air and the three of them ran to the shelter as airplanes flew above them, dropping bombs. The airplanes belonged to the Allies—the United States, Great Britain, and the U.S.S.R.—Germany's enemies.

Raoul bought a ticket for a train leaving the very next day. As Nina guessed, no seats were available. The train was crowded with German soldiers who had been home on leave. Now they were being sent back to Hungary.

Raoul put his knapsack down in the middle of the aisle and used it as a seat. Inside that sack were all the "weapons" he had packed to save lives: practical clothes to wear during the day and a dress-up suit to wear at night. He was wearing an old trench coat and a jaunty hat. Last of all, he bought and packed an old handgun. "I don't think I could ever use it," he told his mother. "But I might need to call someone's bluff." Now, as he sat among all these soldiers with big machine guns, he knew his little gun wouldn't do much good. His wits were his best weapon, along with the carefully folded piece of paper he held in his hands.

On that piece of paper were the names of people who might help him: important people in the Hungarian government; diplomats from other countries; Jewish leaders; and people who pretended to be Nazis but secretly worked against them.

Whenever any of the soldiers looked at Raoul, he smiled at them and nodded. Most of them were still teenagers. None of them suspected that the young man in the trench coat was reading a list of their secret enemies. As the train rolled through Germany and Czechoslovakia, Raoul went over the list until he knew all the names by heart. Then he tore it into little pieces. No one else would ever know the names he had just read.

As his train crossed the border from Czechoslovakia into Hungary, it passed a different kind of train packed full of thousands of people. The men, women, and children on that train had no seats or even any knapsacks to sit on.

They had nothing to eat or drink, no room to move, hardly any to breathe. They were country people. The children had once gone to school, played with their toys and their friends, sang songs, gone to the movies.

Now they were going to die. Raoul had come too late to save them. There was no one to stop their train.

10.

The Adventure Begins

Raoul was up all night on the train. But when he arrived in Budapest, he hired a taxi to take him straight to the Swedish Legation.

Raoul had always loved this lively city. The Danube River ran through the center of town separating the hills of wealthy Buda from middle-class Pest. The Swedish Legation was on one of the hills of Buda. From the taxi, the streets of the city looked very different than they had when he'd visited the year before. Small streets, which always seemed old and mysterious, still wound over the hills of the city. The wide boulevards had been lined with elegant, historic buildings. Now, some of the proud old buildings were nothing more than rubble as a result of the bombing, and the stately old hotels weren't hotels any longer. Now they flew red and black flags with "spider crosses," Nazi swastikas. It was easy to spot the members of the dreaded SS. Their crisp, shiny black uniforms and boots stood out on summer streets.

A few teenagers in uniforms were also on the streets. They were members of the Arrow Cross, Hungarian boys who went to Nazi-style meetings and rallies. The people on the street looked at them with disgust.

As Raoul looked around, the taxi swerved. A ten-year-old girl with dark hair walking quickly, looking at the ground, didn't see the car until she stepped in front of it. When the taxi honked, she looked up quickly. Raoul saw two things: she was wearing a bright yellow star, and she was crying.

"Look out, you dirty Jew-girl!" yelled the driver. "They're always in such a hurry because they're only allowed out of their houses between two and five in the afternoon. Such trouble! Why, they'd run the country if they had the chance!"

"Says who?"

"Where have you been? The Nazi radio programs say it all the time."

"Have you ever known any Jewish people?" asked Raoul.

"Yes. Before the war, why, my dentist and my lawyer were both Jewish. And my baker. We were all great friends. Now I know better."

"Do you really believe that your baker wants to take over the country? And that little girl, too?"

The driver looked at Raoul suspiciously in the mirror. "Mister," he said, "I believe whatever I have to believe to live through this war."

The taxi pulled up to the Swedish Legation.

Raoul paid the man and got out.

The Swedish Legation was a handsome stone building with the bright blue and yellow flag of Sweden flying proudly outside. On this afternoon it was surrounded by hundreds of people standing in the hot sun. Rich and poor, old and young, they all shared the same haunted, hunted look. Many of them wore a yellow star sewed onto their clothes.

When they saw Raoul going into the legation, a thin man with gray hair touched his arm. "Can you help us?" he asked. "We've come for passports. We've waited so long, and now it's nearly five o'clock. We'll have to go home empty-handed."

"Please help us," said a young mother with her baby in her arms.

"I must go inside," Raoul said gently. "Even if you don't get a passport today, don't worry. Come back tomorrow."

"That's what they said to my son," the old man said. "He's a lawyer. But he was just taken away to a camp outside the city!"

"I've been sent to help you," Raoul said. "The Swedes and the Americans care about you. Don't lose hope. The world hasn't forgotten you!"

The people stared after Raoul as he walked past. Most people said to them, "I'm sorry. I can't help you." This man said, "I've come to help." The radio said, "No one cares about you." This man said, "You haven't been forgotten."

They didn't want to get their hopes up. After all, what could one man do against all those soldiers?

II.

At the Legation

Inside the Swedish Legation, the young man asked for Minister Danielsson. A woman pointed into an office. Ivan Danielsson, who was in charge of the legation, was a handsome, middle-aged man who looked very important.

"Hello, I'm Raoul Wallenberg," Raoul said.

"Yes, yes. I know who you are and why you've come. As you can see, we're very, very busy. We can use your help. Mr. Anger will fill you in."

Raoul already knew Per Anger from Sweden and had seen him more recently when Raoul's business brought him to Hungary. He was a young man with dark hair and eyes that would laugh if something was funny. But things hadn't seemed funny for a long time.

"The people waiting outside are waiting for these," Per said when he met with Raoul. He pulled out a piece of paper. It was a document stating that the person who had it was going to move to Sweden after the war and was already protected by the country of Sweden.

"Who can have these?" asked Raoul.

"Only people who have relatives in Sweden," said Per.

"How many passes are you giving out?"

"The Hungarian ruler, Admiral Horthy, will allow forty-five hundred."

Raoul thought a minute. "This is a very good idea," he said. "But it's not enough. We have to save more than forty-five hundred people. I have an idea for another kind of pass."

"We must be careful of Admiral Horthy—"

"I'll talk to him."

Per looked at Raoul in amazement. He had just walked in and already he was planning to talk to the ruler!

"The new Schutzpasse will look different. I know the Germans. They respect things that look fancy. We'll print it in Swedish colors, blue and yellow, and put the king's three royal crowns in gold. It must have the person's picture on it. The soldiers can't think it's just a piece of paper. It must look very important."

Raoul saw Per's surprised look. "Forgive me for jumping right in," he said, "but there is so much to do. I've read the reports. Can you bring me up-to-date? What's happening here in Budapest?"

"No good news, I'm afraid. The Jewish people have tried to reach their families and friends in the countryside. But they've all been taken from their homes. Last week, the Nazis rounded up fifteen hundred Jews right here in Budapest. Many of them were reporters or lawyers. Some were arrested for no reason at all. Their star was pinned on wrong or something silly like that. These people are all in a camp just outside the city."

"Can't we get them out?"

"We don't believe Admiral Horthy will let anything happen to the innocent people of Budapest." Per looked

Schutzpasse. (Photography by Thomas Veres)

around. Then he said quietly, "But I am worried. Colonel Adolph Eichmann is in town. Have you heard of him?"

"Yes," Raoul answered, also quietly. "He's the Nazi in charge of the Einsatzkommando, the troops who kill Jewish people. If he's here, there's no time to spare. First, we'll call a meeting of all the neutral legations in town. We have to work together. Then I'll talk to Admiral Horthy in person. I have a letter to him from the king. Third, I must talk to the Jewish leaders. If evil men are united to kill people, we must be united to save them."

"I'm afraid it will take more than blue and yellow passes and a meeting," sighed Per. "Colonel Eichmann has some nasty tricks up his sleeve."

Raoul shook his arm. "Why, I think I have a few tricks up mine as well," he said. "And I have a very long sleeve."

Before he left the legation office that afternoon, Raoul went to see Minister Danielsson again.

"Do you have any news on the people in the country?" he asked. "I've promised a man named Lauer that I would try to find his family. He has one little niece who was just learning to talk last time I was here." Raoul smiled as he remembered the Lauers' baby. She'd clapped her hands and laughed whenever Raoul picked her up.

Minister Danielsson looked at Raoul. He picked up a report from his desk. "You might want to read these."

Raoul went back to his office. He sat alone at his desk. The report was called The Auschwitz Protocols. *Protocol* means how things are done. Auschwitz was the name of the busiest Nazi death camp in Poland. These reports came from people who had managed to escape from Auschwitz.

Raoul knew he wouldn't like the report, and he was right. It told how thousands and thousands of people were killed by poison gas. Thousands more were shot to death. Those were the lucky ones. Others were tortured before they died. The guards found some prisoners who could play musical instruments. They made them play loudly to cover up the people's screams.

Most of the people killed in Auschwitz were Jews. But many others were sent there as well whose only crime was daring to speak out and protest against what the Nazis were doing.

Then Raoul read another report. It revealed that before the war, 750,000 Jewish people lived in Hungary. Since then more than half had been put into the camps. During the last month, they had been sent to Auschwitz. In all likelihood, they were already dead.

Raoul put the paper down. He remembered Mrs. Lauer's family. The mother had always been happy, laughing and singing as she prepared dinner. Her husband would pretend to be angry that she sang so loud. But when she stopped, he would sing twice as loud as his wife. And the baby. Who would kill a baby with such sparkling brown eyes?

The report made him very, very angry. Slowly he stood up to go. He needed some sleep. Tomorrow he had a lot of work to do.

12.

Castle on a Hill

As soon as he could, Raoul went to see the Hungarian leader, Admiral Miklos Horthy.

The admiral lived in the royal castle on Castle Hill. Raoul was shown into an elegant room. Admiral Horthy sat behind a very big desk. He had once been strong, a war hero, but now he was old. Raoul gave him the letter from King Gustav V of Sweden. In the letter the king said he'd heard what was happening to the Jews in Hungary. He asked the admiral to stop allowing such horrible things to happen.

Admiral Horthy was impressed to receive a letter from the king of Sweden. He looked up at Raoul.

"You know I've told the Nazis to leave our people alone," he said. "And you also know the Nazis don't always listen to me."

"Then perhaps you need to speak more loudly," said Raoul. "The war will be over soon and the whole world will judge what has happened. If they hear you have allowed the murder of thousands of women and children, things will not go well for you."

Admiral Horthy seemed very tired when he spoke. "Mr. Wallenberg, things haven't gone well for me for a long time.

43

But tell His Majesty the King I was glad to get his letter, and I will do what I can."

Next, Raoul went to see the leaders of the Jewish Council on Sip Street. The leaders were older men. Most of the younger men had already been sent away to "work camps."

When Raoul reached the council, he found the room filled with people waiting to speak to someone in charge. He went to the desk. "I'm Wallenberg, Swedish Legation," he said. "I must speak to Mr. Samu Stern on a matter of some importance."

"Yes, yes, I'll tell him," said the man at the desk.

Raoul stood by one of the tall windows. He waited. And waited. The useless waste of time was making him frustrated and angry. Suddenly he felt a hand on his shoulder. He turned to find a young man, about his own age, grinning at him.

"Raoul, what the devil are you doing here? Haven't you heard we're in the middle of a war?"

"Laszlo!" Raoul answered with a smile. "I should have known you'd be in the thick of things!"

Laszlo Peto hardly looked different than he had that summer fifteen years ago when the two boys had stayed in the same hostel in Thonon-les-Bains, France.

"I'm with the Swedish Legation," Raoul told his old friend. "I have an urgent message for the council."

"Just a moment," Laszlo said, and he disappeared.

Within minutes, someone came and whispered to the man at the desk. The man stood up. In a booming voice he said, "Everyone must leave at once! Now! The council has an urgent meeting with the Swedish Legation!"

The room cleared quickly. The men who were the leaders of the Jewish Council remained and sat at a table. Laszlo pulled back a chair for Raoul.

Laszlo said, "Raoul Wallenberg, First Secretary of the Swedish Legation, this is Mr. Samu Stern, head of the council. And this is my father, Dr. Erno Peto. Father, don't you remember me talking about this fellow? We spent the summer together in France when we were teenagers. He wasn't as good with the French girls as I was, but then, no one was. If there's one thing I know, it's that Raoul's a good man. We can trust him with our lives."

"Anyone we trust these days, we trust with our lives," said Laszlo's father.

The men at the council looked at Raoul thoughtfully. "Forgive my suspicion," Mr. Stern said, "but these days everyone says, 'I am on your side. Trust me.' Admiral Horthy says this. Even Colonel Eichmann says this. 'Trust me,' they say. Then thousands of people die."

"I have a letter from Rabbi Marcus Ehrenpreis in Stockholm," Raoul said. "His letter will tell you why I am here."

Mr. Stern took the letter and read it carefully. The other leaders read it, too. Nobody spoke for a minute.

"Young Mr. Wallenberg, what do you want from us?" asked Dr. Peto.

"I've been sent to help you, but I also need your help," Raoul said. "The Nazis have many spies. We must have spies, too. If we share our information, we will be able to do much more."

"Thank you for coming," said Samu Stern. "We'll think about what you've said."

Laszlo left the council room with Raoul. When they were outside, the two friends threw their arms around each other. "It's sure good to see you!" said Laszlo. "I want to know what you've been up to since I saw you, you old dog. But first let's take a walk."

The two friends walked through town to the muddy Danube River, where they could make sure no one was close enough to hear them as they talked.

"What you said back there was right," said Laszlo. "We do have spies of our own. It would be good to share information. For starters, my family knows Admiral Horthy's son. I have his private phone number. If we need to get through to Admiral Horthy right away, this is how we do it.

"Also, there is an Underground. Colonel Eichmann must believe that the Jewish Council is doing what he wants. The old men you talked to stay in sight. But there are young men and women who are out of sight, working secretly. We don't always know what they're doing, but we can contact them.

"Last, we know some officers in the Nazi party who can be bribed into helping us. When the time comes, I'll tell you who they are."

"Thank you, Laszlo," Raoul said. "If we're going to save anyone, we must all work together."

"I want you to come to dinner at my father's house next week," Laszlo said. "When he's talked to you, he'll know he can trust you."

The two men shook hands warmly. "I'll see you next week, then," said Raoul.

13.

Section C

Back at the Swedish Legation, Raoul found many people waiting in line. "Everybody in Budapest is here!" a tired worker said to him.

At the head of the line, a young woman stood at the desk where a clerk was taking the names of people who wanted a pass.

"But you must give me one!" she said. "My life depends on it!"

"What's the trouble?" asked Raoul.

"This young woman has no ties to Sweden at all," said the man at the desk. "She can't even say 'please' and 'thank you' in Swedish."

"You don't understand," the woman cried to Raoul. "My name is Susanna. My husband was a writer for the newspaper. He's been arrested and taken to the camp outside the city. My neighbor said the soldiers came back looking for me. My only hope is to have a Swedish pass!"

"But I've told you," the clerk said, "you have no ties to Sweden."

"Can you type?" asked Raoul.

"Yes. I've written some newspaper stories myself."

"She has a tie to Sweden now," Raoul told the man at the desk. "She works for the Swedish Legation."

Raoul Wallenberg in the Ulloi Street office, November 26, 1944. (Photography by Thomas Veres)

"Thank you!" said the woman.

Raoul had a glint in his eye. "For 'thank you,' we Swedes say *tak*," he said.

The woman smiled at the clerk. "*Tak*," said the newest Swede.

"Come back this way and find a desk. We're starting a new section of the legation, Section C, to issue passes."

Raoul looked at the woman. Her hair was long and red. Her dress had been a good one but now was well worn. She wore a jacket. On the front of the jacket was pinned the yellow star.

"First thing, take off your star."

Susanna was surprised. "Why? When the Nazis said we had to wear it, the Jewish Council told us to wear it with pride. It isn't in style," she smiled, "but it won't kill us."

"I'm afraid that's where you're wrong," Raoul said gently. "It tells the Nazis who their 'enemy' is right away. I plan to make it very difficult for them to find their 'enemies.' "

The woman looked at him for a minute. Then she unpinned her star. "I guess we Swedes don't have to do what the Nazis say," she said.

Susanna went to work immediately typing out passes and starting a file for each person who had one.

Minister Danielsson saw Raoul and came across the room. "I have a gift for you, my boy," he said.

When he stepped aside, Raoul saw his unexpected "gift."

"This is Countess Elizabeth Nako. She is the best secretary in the legation. She's like you, Raoul. She thinks nothing is impossible. So I'm lending her to you."

"*Tak*," said Raoul. Countess Nako was a plump woman

with a pretty face that looked both friendly and determined. She shook hands with Raoul.

"Nice to meet you, Mr. Wallenberg. Let's get to work."

"I think we'll get along very well," he said, smiling.

Raoul hired as many people as he could for Section C. All that mattered was that they were smart and willing to work. Soon his Section C had eighty people and took up one whole floor of the legation.

At two o'clock every afternoon the long line started outside. Before they opened the doors, Raoul turned to his workers. "Listen, all of you," he said. "Help everyone you can. If you have a problem, call me. But most important, you must treat each person like a human being. The Nazis try to tell the Jewish people that they are worthless, that they are dogs, and that there is no hope. We must remind them that they are important. They are people. There is hope.

"The Nazis have given power to evil. We will give power to good!"

"Yes, we will!" agreed the staff.

"All right then. Open the doors. Let our friends come in."

14.

The First Fight

The next Friday Raoul went back to the Jewish Council on Sip Street. He was going to tell them about the meeting of the neutral embassies. But before they could sit down, the door to the street flew open and a ragged boy ran inside. The boy had been running fast, and he was out of breath.

"Who are you?" asked Samu Stern.

The boy shook his head. "Quickly!" he panted.

"Quickly what?" asked Dr. Peto.

"Phone call! Train! Gone!" gasped the boy.

Mr. Stern, the former businessman, stood, and grabbed the boy's shoulders with his very strong hands. "Who is gone?"

"Everyone . . . in the camp . . . outside the city. They're all on a train!"

"When did this happen?" asked Raoul.

"Just an hour ago. Mr. Brody said I was to come here and tell you."

All of the men were now standing. "We must act at once," someone yelled.

"Peto, call Horthy Jr. right away," said Mr. Stern. Dr. Peto hurried away. "We must also call Cardinal Seredi."

"I'll alert all of the legations," said Raoul. He ran out to the car that was waiting for him. "Drive quickly to the Swiss Legation," he said.

When he arrived at the legation's office, Raoul went straight to the office of Swiss Consul Charles Lutz, who looked up from his work in surprise.

"Wallenberg! What are you doing here?"

"Colonel Eichmann has taken everyone from the camp outside the city. They're on a train heading for the border. If that train leaves Hungary, every person on it will be dead!"

"There's no time to waste," Mr. Lutz said. He was as concerned about the situation as Raoul. "Let me see what I can do. Then we must alert the other neutrals at once."

He picked up the phone. "This is the Swiss consul," he said. "I must speak to Admiral Horthy. No, I won't wait. This is an emergency." He waited a minute. "Admiral Horthy? This is Swiss Consul Charles Lutz. Sir, on behalf of my country, I must protest that everyone from the Budapest camp is being sent to their death."

Horthy spoke, then Consul Lutz said, "It doesn't matter that your son has just now told you. You must stop this murder. These are your own citizens. Switzerland will hold you responsible."

Raoul left while Mr. Lutz was still on the phone. He hurried next to the legation from Portugal, then to the legation of Spain. From there he went to the delegation that represented the pope. Raoul made sure that every consul had heard about the train and had called Admiral Horthy to object. Every minute took the train—and thousands of people—closer to the border and closer to their deaths.

Finally, he hurried back to the Swedish Legation. As he entered, everyone in Section C looked up. "Is it true?" a man asked.

"Yes," said Raoul.

"They're all gone?" asked an old woman.

Susanna ran up to Raoul. "But my husband Paul?"

"Come," said Raoul. Susanna held on to his arm as he walked to Danielsson's office. All the workers stopped what they were doing.

"So it is true?" asked Minister Danielsson. "They've emptied the camp?"

Raoul nodded. Mr. Danielsson picked up the telephone. "Give me Horthy," he said in a commanding voice.

The whole legation was so quiet that the drone of a fly could be heard. "Admiral Horthy, this is Minister Danielsson. Yes, that is what I am calling about." Ivan Danielsson listened a minute. "Then there is nothing for me to say," he said. He hung up the phone.

Then he looked at the dozens of people who were watching him.

"Admiral Horthy knows that we protest. He sent Captain Lullay to find the train." He took a breath. "The train was stopped inside Hungary. The people are all right. They are coming back!"

All of the Swedes—old and "new"—gave a cheer.

"Such a thing has never happened to me!" sputtered Adolph Eichmann. He was talking to his helper, Dieter Wisliceny. Colonel Eichmann's face was red, and his eyes were burning with fury. As he talked, he marched back and forth across the floor in his shiny black boots.

"Turn the train around! Who do they think they're dealing with?"

Dieter had never seen the colonel in such a rage. He knew there would be trouble now.

15.

"No More"

"Eichmann has sent orders for all the members of the Jewish Council to be in his office by eight-thirty on Monday morning," said Laszlo to Raoul as they were eating dinner.

"I wonder what he's planning," said Raoul.

"I don't know. Probably he'll make them wait a long time. Then he'll come in and yell and rant and rave. Maybe he'll demand more mattresses."

The two men laughed, but it hadn't been funny when Adolph Eichmann had first demanded the mattresses. When he first came to town, he had called the council together. The men all sat down while Colonel Eichmann paced around. "You must obey me," he said. "Then you will come to no harm. You must wear a yellow star on your clothes at all times. You must give me your property for safekeeping. And don't bother to speak any other languages. I understand whatever you say.

"Our German soldiers need a few things, and I have told them that you, our friends, will be happy to give them as gifts. This is what you must bring me tomorrow. Crystal glasses. Silverware. Mops and pails. Typewriters. Perfume. A painting by the artist named Watteau. And, we would like a piano. Thank you."

The men knew they were in grave danger. They collected the items that Eichmann had wanted, and he called them back the next day.

"Thank you, gentlemen. Here is the rest of my list. We need three hundred mattresses and six hundred blankets. By tomorrow."

"But, Colonel," objected Mr. Stern, "we're in the middle of a war. We can't get so many things in one day."

Colonel Eichmann exploded. "Listen, if I can figure out how to kill ten thousand Jews in ten minutes, you can find blankets!"

Raoul and Laszlo knew he would not want blankets this time. They were afraid to find out what he did want.

"Please call me as soon as you hear what happens at the meeting," said Raoul.

Early on Monday morning the members of the council went to Eichmann's headquarters. He had taken over a beautiful old hotel. A Nazi soldier showed them to the meeting room. When they were all there, the soldiers closed the door and stood outside it. Colonel Eichmann was not there by eight-thirty, or nine o'clock, or even by ten or eleven o'clock.

Finally Dr. Peto knocked on the door. When the soldier opened it, Peto asked for the colonel.

"Colonel Eichmann is busy," the man snapped. "Are you tired of waiting for him? Do you have something better to do?" The soldiers laughed and closed the door again.

The council members waited all afternoon. They waited all evening. Finally, at 7:30 P.M., the door banged open and Adolph Eichmann strode inside. He was wearing a large grin.

Adolph Eichmann, the Nazi in charge of the Einsatzkom-mando, the troops who killed Jews. (AP/Wide World Photos)

"So sorry to keep you all waiting. It was hard to fit everyone from the camps onto one train! But it's done." He looked at his watch. "And just now the train has crossed the border. One thousand two hundred and twenty people have left Hungary for good. There's nothing you can do. You may go now, gentlemen. Thank you for coming by. Good night."

Susanna came and stood outside Raoul's office. It was late at night, but many people were still working. "So it's true, they've deported the people from the camp?"

"I'm afraid so," said Raoul. He saw she was holding a framed photo against her chest. "Is that your husband?"

"Yes, it's Paul," she said. She handed him the picture. A handsome young man with brown hair and friendly eyes looked back at him. "I've been in love with him since I was twelve," Susanna said. Then she laughed. "He didn't know he loved me until he was old, twenty at least. He said when the war was over we'd have a proper honeymoon. In Berlin." She tried to smile. "He was always kidding." Her smile wavered. She turned away quickly so Raoul wouldn't see her cry.

Raoul sat for a minute, unable to work. He had come here to save people, and twelve hundred had just been sent to their deaths. He did not like to lose any more than did Adolph Eichmann.

He knew there was one more task he had to do yet today. He had been putting it off because it was so hard. He took out stationery on his big desk and picked up a pen.

"Dear Mother," he wrote. "Please invite Mr. Lauer to dinner. I haven't the heart to tell him myself. His wife's family have all been deported and probably killed." He stopped. Then he added, "Even the little child."

He thought again about what Adolph Eichmann was doing. "No more," he whispered. "No more!"

16.

Safe Houses

Raoul met his friend Laszlo again on the walk along the Danube. It was important that no one hear what they said to one another. Before the war, boys and girls used to hold hands and walk slowly by the lazy river. Now passersby looked over their shoulders.

Raoul spoke first. "You said you knew of Nazis who were willing to help us. What have you heard about Lieutenant Colonel Laszlo Ferenczy?"

"He knows the Germans are losing the war," said Laszlo. "He says he's willing to help us because he's a good person, but we all know better. He's trying to save his own skin. The council members despise him because he's such a liar. But we work with him because he can save lives."

"I believe I'll pay a call on Colonel Ferenczy," said Raoul.

"Get what you can from him. But don't trust him."

A few days later Raoul entered the headquarters of the gendarmerie, the Hungarian police from the countryside who'd come to Budapest to help with the deportations. With him were two of his Hungarian friends, Elizabeth and Alexander Kasser, who worked for the Red Cross. At the desk, Mrs. Kasser spoke Hungarian: "Mr. Wallenberg has come to see Colonel Ferenczy. He knows we are coming."

"I'll tell him," said the private.

Hundreds of gendarmes in brown uniforms hurried up and down the halls. Colonel Ferenczy was in charge of them all. He was the link between Admiral Horthy's government and Colonel Eichmann's Nazi command. It was his job to see that all the Jews from the countryside were shipped off to death camps. He was doing his job very well.

The private came back in a minute. "Follow me," he said.

He led them back into the section of the building "for authorized personnel only," ushered them into Ferenczy's office, and told them to wait. Mrs. Kasser was a little nervous because Raoul was telling very funny jokes about Ferenczy in German. She knew the colonel didn't speak German, but it made her nervous just the same.

At last the colonel came. Raoul held out his hand. "Wallenberg. Swedish Legation."

Ferenczy began yelling at them in Hungarian. He said nasty things about Jewish people. Then he said nasty things about them for helping people. Mrs. Kasser knew that Raoul wasn't yet fluent in Hungarian and purposely didn't translate everything the colonel said.

When he was done, Raoul pretended nothing was wrong.

"Sir, as you know, Jewish people can no longer own buildings here in Budapest. You have taken most of their houses away from them."

"So what?" he answered.

"Now you have many more houses than you need, but you're low on money. I'm willing to buy houses from you for cash."

"And what do you plan to do with these houses?"

"We know that the Nazis want to get rid of the Jews in Hungary, and we're happy to help. Many of them have gotten passes so they can move to Sweden. They can live in these houses until they are able to move. We'll do you a favor. We'll get them out of your way."

"I see what you're trying to do, Mr. Wallenberg," Ferenczy said.

"It's all legal. Horthy has approved the passes. The Swedish minister has personally signed each one."

"How much money can you pay for the houses?"

"We'll pay you well," Raoul said and named a price.

"I can spare three buildings. You can fit six hundred and fifty of your new 'Swedes' there. But you must bring me cash."

Mr. Kasser spoke next. "You know the Red Cross will make reports after the war," he said. "We'll tell who helped us and who did not. If you will sell some houses to the Red Cross, it will look good for you."

"Yes, yes. You may also buy three. Now go, all of you. Before I change my mind."

The men gave serious bows to each other. Raoul and the Kassers said nothing as they walked from the building. They walked down the steps outside and around the corner. Then, as soon as no one could see them, they put their arms around each other and danced a jig.

"We're on our way." Raoul grinned, and the Kassers gave a cheer.

Raoul also persuaded some well-to-do Jews to sign their houses over to Sweden for safekeeping until after the war. He put large blue and yellow Swedish flags outside each one. The other embassies followed Raoul's example. The gendarmes didn't bother the people who lived in these

Returning from trains to safe houses along Jozsef Krt. (Joseph Boulevard). Taken from a car driven by Vilmos Langfelder. (Photography by Thomas Veres)

buildings. Finally families had somewhere to live, somewhere they felt safe.

At the legation, Section C grew quickly. Raoul had hired four hundred people. Now there was not enough room for them all in the legation's office, so Raoul used Mr. Olsen's money to buy the buildings on either side. He set up offices in Pest as well. Each day hundreds of people, trying to prove any link to Sweden at all, lined up hoping to obtain a Swedish pass.

One day Raoul saw that his secretary, Countess Nako, looked troubled.

"What's wrong, Elizabeth?" he said.

"I feel bad for the people who don't get passes," she said. "Many of them don't know anybody in Sweden. Some do, but they don't have the strength to stand in line for hours. It's good that some people are in protected houses. Yet many people aren't safe and have nothing to eat. They feel hopeless, as if no one cares for them."

Raoul had been thinking the same thing. He knew it was part of Colonel Eichmann's plan to make people feel hopeless because without hope there was no reason to fight back.

"Vilmos, let's go," Raoul said to his driver. Vilmos Lang-felder was an engineer from an important family. Because he was part Jewish, he was marked for death. Now he drove a legation car for Raoul. The Swedish flags on the outside of the car meant that legally everyone inside the car—Vilmos, too—was Swedish.

Together Vilmos and Raoul drove from Buda across the river to Pest. Raoul got out in front of one of the Swedish protected houses.

As he strode into the entry hall of one building, people stopped what they were doing and gathered around him. On the stairs he spotted an older man with kind, thoughtful eyes.

"Saul, I've come to talk to you. You're a doctor, aren't you?"

The man looked surprised. "I was until the Nazis forbade me to work."

"Good. I need you to run our new hospital."

By now, many people were on the stairs and in the hallway. "Listen, all of you," Raoul said. "Now that you're here, you're safe. Since you're Swedes, you don't have to wear yellow stars and you may walk around town any time you like. But you haven't been freed from Colonel Eichmann's control just so you can go to the theater.

"We've helped you so you can help others. Many of your friends and relatives are sick and frightened and have nothing to eat. Let's do something about it. I need your skills. I need what you know. Before the war, before your jobs were taken away, many of you were doctors, nurses, or dentists. We need you now. We're opening a clinic and a hospital. Were any of you builders?"

"Yes!"

"Here!"

"I was!"

"Good. You'll help us repair the buildings. Now, who were bakers and cooks? You'll run the soup kitchens. Who can sew? We'll make and mend warm clothing for winter. And children? Who's good at sneaking food and material past the Arrow Cross?"

A shout went up. They were all good at that.

"We have our work cut out for us. Colonel Eichmann is very organized. But who will be more organized?"

"We will," they answered.

"Who will work harder?"

"We will!"

"And who will help others live through this war?"

"We will!" the people said.

17.

A Dangerous Farewell

The hot August sun glared off shiny black helmets as row after row of SS soldiers marched through the streets of Budapest. The tromp-tromp-tromp of their boots sounded like the roar of floodwaters broken out of a dam. People on the street stopped to stare at them. Many of them then hurried away. A few cheered.

Raoul shook his head. "I don't believe it," he said to his friend Hugo Wohl. "The Nazis are losing the war. You'd think they'd send every single soldier to fight their enemies. Instead they send them here, to a country on their side, because there are Jews left in one city."

"Do you think the rumors are true? The deportations are starting again?" Mr. Wohl asked. Before the war, he had run a large radio station. Now he helped Raoul run Section C. A Swedish pass had saved his life. "They say Colonel Eichmann will send thousands of people to the brick factory. From there, he'll put them on trains to the gas chamber."

"Yes," said Raoul as they reached his Studebaker with Swedish flags on either side of the hood. "I'm sure Colonel Eichmann is planning to kill as many people as he can. That's why he's marching his men through town. He wants people to be too afraid to fight back. If we can only find out when he's going to start, we can come up with a plan."

Mr. Wohl knew when Raoul said "*we* can come up with a plan," it meant *he* would.

Just then there was a knocking on the window of the backseat. Outside stood Raoul's friend Laszlo Peto. He was out of breath.

"Laszlo! What are you doing here?" Raoul asked.

"I have to talk to you," Laszlo said.

"Get in," Raoul said, and he opened the door to pull him inside. "Go!" the Swede said to Vilmos. As they moved through the streets, he turned back to his friend. "What on earth were you doing so close to that blasted parade?"

"My father and the other leaders of the council were arrested last night," Laszlo said. "They even got Mr. Stern off his sickbed. He's seventy years old, he has pneumonia, and they took him off in the middle of the night."

"Where are they? Have you heard from them? Are they all right?"

"They were taken to Gestapo headquarters on Schwab Hill and tortured. My father had a letter from you in his coat. He tried to tear it up, but they found it. The Gestapo knows you're working to save Jews, Raoul. It may not be safe for you here much longer."

"Thanks for the warning, my friend. But what happened to your father?"

"After they beat them for several hours, they let them go. It was a warning of what will happen if they don't do what they're told. But that's not why I came to find you."

"Why did you come?"

"Colonel Ferenczy says the deportations are ready to start. He knows the date. He's ready to talk."

Raoul remembered Colonel Ferenczy. What did he want now? If it was more money, as he'd wanted for the houses, Raoul had it. But Raoul knew that very soon something would be worth much more than money: food. As supply lines were cut off, there would be no way to get food into the city. Raoul had already started secretly buying as much food as possible. He would use most of it to feed hungry people. Some of the food he'd trade for things that were even more precious—like time, information, lives.

"Let's go visit our friend the colonel," Raoul said.

Samu Stern and Laszlo's father were already waiting at the Jewish Council building when Raoul and Laszlo arrived. It was clear neither of them had slept. Mr. Stern had a long cut above his eye and Dr. Peto had bruises on his hands.

"If you ask me, Ferenczy is a dog, but we need his help," said Mr. Stern.

No sooner had he said this than the door swung open, and Ferenczy burst into the room. "Keep guard outside the door," he snapped at the gendarmes who had come with him. "Don't let anyone in or out until I'm done speaking with our friends." He spit out the last word.

When the door closed, his voice dropped to a whisper. "I don't have much time," he said. "All of you Jews are in grave danger."

"I noticed that when I was dragged from my home for a friendly visit with the Gestapo," muttered Dr. Peto.

"Quiet!" the colonel said. "Do you want my help or not?"

"You're the only man who can help us," said Mr. Stern, trying to calm him down. "But may we ask why this change of heart?"

68

"I'm not a man who likes killing. It was my job. But the war will be over soon."

"The answer to the question you're going to ask is yes," said Raoul. "We at the neutral legations are keeping very clear notes on who committed crimes during the war and who stopped crimes. I'll make a careful note that you helped us stop the new deportations. What would help us most is knowing the date they will begin."

"You're right. Herr Eichmann has been told to start again. The date he has chosen is . . ." Ferenczy looked at each man, making sure they understood how much he was helping them. "August 25."

"August 25? But that's hardly a week away," Laszlo cried.

"I've done what I can," Ferenczy said. As he opened the door, he yelled, "Those are my clear instructions. I expect them to be obeyed."

Moments after they heard his car pull away, Raoul rushed out the door himself. Laszlo had seen the look on his face. He couldn't help smiling, even though he knew the news was bad. He also knew Raoul had a plan.

Raoul went straight to the Swedish Legation building and bounded up the wide marble steps to Minister Danielsson's office. He was dictating letters to his secretary. When he saw Raoul out of breath, he waved her out and closed the door.

"What is it?" he asked.

"Deportations start again next Friday," the young man said.

Danielsson stared at him. "What do you propose to do?"

"Admiral Horthy must know by now that the Axis Powers are losing, and losing badly. If he can stand up to

69

Raoul Wallenberg in the Ulloi Street office. Note the candles: electricity was unreliable. (Photography by Thomas Veres)

the Nazis now, it might buy us the time we need to hold out until the war ends. Phone calls won't be enough this time. We need something very official in writing. It must show that we know what's going on and that the admiral's actions will matter very much when this war is over."

"And who's going to sign this paper?"

Raoul smiled. "You are, for a start, sir. We'll have a meeting on Monday night attended by ambassadors from every neutral legation still in Budapest. Horthy will know he must answer for his actions—to four nations and the pope."

Danielsson shook his head. He knew he should feel annoyed that this brash young man was ordering him around. But so much was at stake.

He reached for his calendar. "What time on Monday?" he asked.

On the morning of Tuesday, August 22, Admiral Horthy sat at his desk in the castle on the hill, their letter in front of him. He knew the deportations were to begin by the end of the week. His friends from the Jewish Council had told him that. Colonel Ferenczy had even arranged a secret meeting to give him the information in person. Did he dare go against Germany and forbid it from taking the Budapest Jews? They were, after all, Hungarians. His own citizens.

Admiral Horthy gave a long sigh. Once he was willing to take risks to stand up for what he believed. But that was before his oldest son, Istvan, had been killed in the war. Now very little seemed worth fighting for. Still, he had to think of his second son, Miklos, who was urging him to stop the Nazis.

The admiral looked again at the very official letter on his desk. It said that everyone knew what "deportation to labor service" really meant. It said if he allowed this to happen, Hungary would no longer be counted among the civilized nations of the world. It said he was held responsible to four different nations and the pope.

Meanwhile, Adolph Eichmann was a very happy man. It was hard to believe that little more than ten years before he was selling fuel oil. Now he held the fate of thousands of people in his hands. He hoped that Ger-

71

many would win the war, but even if it didn't, thanks to him, Europe would be *Judenrein*—free of Jews. The last ones alive were in Hungary. Eichmann had sent so many long trains crammed with people to Auschwitz each day that the head of the camp had to make a special trip to see him. "Slow down!" he'd said. "I can't possibly kill people as fast as you send them to me!"

Now the camp commander would have to get his "showers" ready again. More than one hundred thousand people from Budapest would soon be on their way. Then he would have destroyed the last large community of Jews in Europe. The very last!

His telephone buzzed and he picked it up. "Colonel Ferenczy is here to see you," said his aide.

Eichmann strode to his door and threw it open. The halls were filled with activity. Knowing that all these people obeyed him was a good feeling. When he saw Colonel Ferenczy, he clicked his heels together. "Heil Hitler!"

"Heil Hitler!" Ferenczy returned.

"Is everything in order?" Colonel Eichmann asked.

"Let's talk in your office," Ferenczy said.

Eichmann closed the door behind them. "What's your report?"

"Not good, I'm afraid."

"What are you talking about?" Eichmann demanded.

"Admiral Horthy refuses to allow the deportations."

Eichmann became so angry he began to shake.

"Refuses to allow?"

"Yes, Colonel."

"What are you talking about? He's brought his own men in from the countryside to help in the operation."

Ferenczy's eyes narrowed. "He's betrayed us, Colonel.

He's brought nineteen thousand gendarmes to Budapest, and now he says they'll use force to stop us."

Adolph Eichmann couldn't remember when he'd been so angry. He'd been betrayed by that sniveling old man in the castle. Well. If Admiral Horthy wanted to see force, he'd show him force. The streets would run with Hungarian blood.

"This isn't over yet," Eichmann said. "Get my secretary in here. I'll wire Berlin right away for permission to go ahead at all costs. Now, go. Get out!"

Work in Section C of the Swedish Legation came to a standstill. Raoul stood in the center of a cluster of people who had turned on a large brown radio. It was illegal to listen to the Allies' broadcast, but it was the only way to get the news.

Hugo Wohl came puffing up the stairs. "Well? Is it true?" he asked.

"Shhh!" said everyone, almost at once.

Just then, the station came in loud and clear. "Stunning Allied victory!" the announcer said. "The country of Romania has fallen to the Allied forces!"

"Germany has lost again," someone whispered. "The war will surely be over soon!"

As they strained to hear more news, new footfalls were heard coming up the stairs. It was another young man who worked for Section C.

"Did you hear? Romania is liberated. And the news is even better from across town. Germany needs Hungary's help now more than ever. They want to keep Horthy happy. Colonel Eichmann has gotten word straight from Himmler in Berlin. All deportations are called off!"

A rousing cheer went up. Raoul was as happy as everyone else. Some started singing and dancing. Some threw papers up in the air. Raoul did a little singing himself. Yet he couldn't help feeling wary.

They'd won this round. But he knew the fight wasn't over.

Across town, Adolph Eichmann stood on the landing strip ready to board a military plane. He wore his crisp black uniform with the blood-red armbands. Under his elbow he carried a crop. He'd never been so furious or so humiliated. He'd been made to look like a fool. Still, he couldn't fight orders from General Himmler. He had to get out of this dirty town where they protected Jews and laughed at Nazis.

When had things started to go wrong? Admiral Horthy was standing up for himself. The neutral nations were making trouble. Even some of the Jews were not doing as they were told.

Eichmann knew one thing for certain. Things had been much better before the arrival of that meddling Swede, Wallenberg. As he marched up the steps onto the airplane heading for Berlin, he looked back out the door and made one promise.

He would be back. And next time, nothing—and no one—would stand in his way.

18.

A Nightmare Comes to Life

Raoul was optimistic. October had come, and it looked as though the end was in sight. During the past three months, he'd worked hard. He'd distributed thousands of Swedish passes, set up hospitals and soup kitchens, moved many new "Swedes" into protected houses, and persuaded the other neutral powers to do the same. Together they'd foiled Eichmann's plan to destroy all the Jews in Budapest.

Raoul had finally gotten people released from "work camps" in the countryside. Hundreds of men came home to their families for the first time in months. Many Jewish citizens were now ripping off the yellow stars that marked them as the "enemy" of their neighbors.

Laughter floated into his office from some workers in Section C, and Raoul smiled at the sound of it. A large stack of passes on his desk was still waiting to be signed, but work was winding down.

He picked up paper and a pen to write his report to Mr. Olsen, the man who had sent him to save the Jews of Budapest. It had been a tricky job, but the worst was over. Or so he thought.

Two weeks later, Miki Horthy was happy. He walked into the castle courtyard and breathed deeply in the crisp autumn air. This was the day he and his father, Admiral Horthy, had planned for many weeks. Today the war would end for Hungary. They had worked out terms of surrender to the Allies. No more bombs exploding over the city. No more shooting on the front. No more life under Germany's rule. Miki and his father hoped the Allies would look more favorably on Hungary if it broke away from Hitler and Germany now, before the war was over.

The young man had one more secret meeting before his father announced the separate peace this very afternoon. Miki's private car pulled up. He gave a short salute to his armed guards and got in. They drove down off the castle hill toward a meeting with people from Yugoslavia who had also shaken off Hitler's iron fist. Miki and his father needed all the allies they could get to make sure the Germans stayed out of Hungary.

Miki's thoughts were interrupted as they came to a roadblock a few blocks from the castle.

As the car stopped, it was suddenly surrounded by hooded men in trench coats. They each wore a yellow star out of spite for the Jews. Their leader was a famous SS colonel, Otto Skorzeny.

There were gunshots. Young Horthy's bodyguards lay bleeding on the ground.

Miki grabbed for his pistol. Before he could reach it, a hooded man opened his door and hit him, hard, on the head. He was unconscious when they wrapped him in a large carpet and dumped him into the trunk of another car.

Moments later that car sped away. The roadblock disappeared. Miki's bodyguards lay bleeding in the street.

Admiral Horthy was a very miserable old man. He looked at the officers and at their soldiers carrying machine guns who surrounded him in a building on the castle grounds. He glanced again at the paper in his hand, which gave full control of his beloved Hungary to Ferenc Szalasi, the leader of the Arrow Cross, the party made up of the hated riffraff of Hungarian society.

"There's no use fighting. German troops have surrounded Budapest. There are giant tanks on the castle lawn. And we have your son. If you don't sign this paper giving full control of Hungary to Mr. Szalasi, you'll never see your son again."

"What will happen to me?" asked Admiral Horthy in a tired voice.

"We think it's time for you to retire. We've picked out a very nice spot in Germany."

Admiral Horthy suddenly felt very old and very ill.

Outside, his own prerecorded message was already playing over the radio. *"Fellow citizens! We won't be Germany's last bloody battleground. We've agreed to stop fighting the Soviet army. The war is over!"*

It was a cruel lie. Hungary's war had just begun.

Tears stung the old man's eyes as he picked up his pen and signed the paper.

Outside, the Germans were ruthlessly taking control of Budapest.

The men in the "Swedish" labor brigade returned from their day of forced labor to report to their synagogue and sign out. The Hungarian army captain who usually met them was gone. German SS men stood in his place.

"It's time for us to go for the day," one man said.

77

"No one's going anywhere," said the SS captain.
He locked the doors with a smile.

In Pest, the Jewish section of town suddenly buzzed with men whose black SS uniforms made them look like thin, deadly wasps. With them were Hungarian teenaged boys. These new recruits had been given smart green uniforms. They had been taught that all Jews must die. Then they were given guns.

The SS and the Arrow Cross went from door to door. They dragged out every Jewish man they could find, whether he was thirteen or ninety-three. "Everyone to the Central Synagogue!" they snarled.

In one of the houses on Teleki Square, some young men home from labor brigades saw what was happening. "This is it. They've come for us. Are we going to let them take us away and kill us without a fight?" asked one.

"Never!" his friends shouted.

Together they raced to the basement. They lifted the floorboards and removed the guns hidden there. When the soldiers pounded on their door, the young men aimed their guns and fired. The SS and the Arrow Cross shot back with machine guns and automatic rifles. Word of their resistance reached German headquarters within minutes. Soon Teleki Square filled with SS soldiers and the Arrow Cross. The young men, badly outnumbered, were all dead within half an hour.

But the soldiers weren't finished.

"So you want to see what happens when someone disobeys us?" screamed a captain. The soldiers went from house to house. They dragged everyone out—young women, old women, old men, little children—more than two hundred in all.

The soldiers shot them all and left them lying in the square. The nightmare had begun.

19.

Get to Work!

The next morning, Raoul hurried toward one of the buildings in Pest that housed the offices of Section C. He'd worked almost all night trying to reach those in power and finding out who was in danger.

He knew the gendarmerie and soldiers were rounding up all the Jewish people. Six thousand men were locked inside the Central Synagogue. Many "Swedish" Jews were in protected houses around the city, but he didn't know how much longer they'd be safe. The rest had been herded into the Jewish "Central Ghetto" in Pest. Hundreds of children were in orphanages without food or clothing.

Raoul knew any Jewish person with Gentile friends had "vanished" into hiding. This was dangerous, for if they were found, their "hosts" would meet the same fate as their Jewish "guests."

Raoul knew about the shooting at Teleki Square. He knew the Germans were having the Jews rounded up for one purpose: to transport them to their deaths. He also knew who was orchestrating this quick and deadly plan.

Adolph Eichmann had returned to Budapest.

For Raoul, his fight with Eichmann had become a personal one. He had trained his staff to work almost as efficiently as Eichmann's. Now he would find out if Section

C could accomplish the task it was set up to do. This was the true test of its dedication and courage.

It was time to get to work. Raoul threw open the door to the Section C office.

It was empty.

Quickly, he went from desk to desk, from one file cabinet to another. They were all locked. His workers were in hiding and they had taken the keys!

He heard a noise and whirled around. Hannah, a teenager who lived in a protected Swedish apartment, stood there.

"Where is everybody?" he asked.

"Hiding," she said, "or arrested."

"Hannah, find everyone you can. Tell them their passes are still good. They're safer here working at the legation than they are hiding, even in safe houses. Round up everyone you can. Tell them to be here by noon."

"I'll try."

"What?"

"Yes. Yes! By noon!"

There was so much to do. Even Raoul's car had been stolen. In the legation garage, he found a rusty bike. He jumped on and started pedaling through the streets of Pest to round up his workers and their keys.

By two o'clock the main Swedish Legation across the river in Buda was a mob scene. Thousands of people had come in a panic, hoping for any kind of help.

Inside, Raoul hurried toward the stairs.

"Raoul?" The voice belonged to Per Anger. Raoul stepped into Anger's office. With Anger was a young man with wavy hair and eyes that betrayed a quick mind.

"Raoul, this is Tom Veres, a photographer, a friend of mine. He could be useful."

"Good," Raoul said, turning to Tom. "As my photographer, you'll document the work we're doing. You'll report directly to me. Do you speak any languages besides Hungarian?"

"English and German," said the surprised young man.

"Great," said Raoul, switching from Hungarian to English. "As you can tell, my Hungarian is only passable. Let's make out your official papers right now. Check in at my office on Ulloi Street each morning. I'll leave word for you with Mrs. Falk, my secretary there."

Raoul nodded and hurried on his way.

As October passed, life in Budapest got worse. Each day it seemed there was news, all of it bad.

"Wallenberg, there you are," said Minister Danielsson, as Raoul made a rare visit to the Buda legation. "Have you heard the radio? The new government is planning to cancel all protective passes. They plan to take away all power from the neutral nations."

Raoul knew without the protection of the passes he could do nothing. Thinking fast, he went to his office and closed the door. Then he placed a telephone call. "Hello, Wallenberg here," he said. "I'd like to speak to the baroness."

During his stay in Budapest, Raoul had made a point of going to many parties. He had met wealthy people, diplomats, government officials, and their wives. He had learned who sided with the Allies and who might be able to help him.

Baroness Elisabeth Kemeny.
(Courtesy of Baroness Elisabeth
Kemeny-Fuchs)

Baron Gabor Kemeny, the
new Hungarian foreign minister.
(Courtesy of Baroness Elisabeth
Kemeny-Fuchs)

Now he needed help.

Raoul had met Baroness Elisabeth Kemeny at a diplomatic reception that she and her husband, Baron Gabor Kemeny, the new Hungarian foreign minister, had given. The baroness was young and high-spirited. She wore her blond hair swept up off her neck, and her lovely gown could no longer hide that she was expecting a baby. She and Raoul found they had much in common. They both spoke English, and they were both concerned about the fate of the Jews.

"Mr. Wallenberg," she said as she picked up the phone.

"Baroness, forgive me if I come right to the point. I've

had some very bad news. You're the only one in Budapest who can help me."

The baroness had never heard his voice so sad. "What's wrong?" she asked.

"There's going to be a government meeting tonight where they're planning to cancel all protective passes. If that happens, I am powerless to help anyone."

"What do you want me to do?"

"Talk to your husband. Explain to him that we have files on every man, woman, and child who has a Swedish pass. If he doesn't honor the passes, he will be responsible for every single one who is hurt or killed. I know you understand and that you feel as I do about the terrible things that are happening. That's why I'm asking for your help. For the sake of thousands of innocent people who will be killed, see what you can do."

"I'll do what I can," she promised, remembering the tattered group of old men, young women, and children she'd seen brutally marched away weeks earlier, carrying everything they owned in rags tied to sticks.

"Where are you taking them?" she had demanded of the Arrow Cross boys who prodded them with guns.

"Don't worry, they're going to work," came the laughing reply.

"What do you think I am, an idiot?" she had asked. "Six-year-old children can't work!"

Now she thought about what Raoul Wallenberg was asking of her and about her handsome husband who wanted to save his beloved Hungary from the Communists fighting their way toward Budapest. Even if it meant that he had to become part of the Szalasi government, he was willing to pay the price.

When Gabor came home that night to his elegant apartment on the hill just below the castle, he could tell something was bothering his wife. "What's wrong, Elisabeth?" he asked.

"Is there a meeting tonight about the protective passes?" she asked.

He was amazed. "How did you know this?"

"Gabor, those passes are the only thing saving thousands of people from death!"

"Thousands of Jews, you mean."

"Jews are people!"

"This is none of your business!"

"You must help. You're the only one in all of Budapest who can help. You're the foreign minister. Make them see the passes must be honored if the new government wants recognition from the foreign nations."

The baron followed his wife into the dining room, where an elegant table was set for dinner. He slammed the door behind them so fiercely that the chandelier rattled above them.

Elisabeth winced. But part of her was glad that he was so angry. It meant that he was being affected by what she said.

"Who put you up to this? Who? That Wallenberg?"

"You know how I feel about killing innocent people."

"My lovely wife, just what is it you want me to do? Stand alone against the whole government? It's impossible."

Elisabeth's mouth went dry. She loved this man. She hated to press him like this. But so many lives were in the balance. She took a deep breath. "Gabor, if you don't do this, I will leave you. I will pack tonight and go home to my mother. You'll never see our child."

Baron Kemeny was furious. Elisabeth never made empty threats. He felt cornered. In blind anger, he grabbed the tablecloth and pulled. Everything—the candles, the food, the crystal, and the china—crashed to the floor. Glass flew everywhere. He stormed out of the house.

At midnight, Elisabeth sat alone by the wireless radio. She was so nervous that it was hard for her to catch her breath.

Finally, the radio blared, "Attention! Attention! This is Foreign Minister Kemeny! The following protective passes must be honored: Three thousand from the Papal Nunzio. Three thousand Swiss. Three thousand Swedish. Anyone holding such a pass is not to be harmed. Repeat! Not to be harmed!"

Elisabeth sighed deeply with relief. She knew, however, her own work to save people was just beginning. To her, a Catholic, Wallenberg seemed like a heroic knight on a crusade. This was one crusade she would join as well.

Even though the Schutzpasses were honored, the new government demanded that all the protected Jews be moved together to a part of the city where there were already some protected houses. Before long there was a strange sight in Pest. Many buildings flew the large flags of other countries like Sweden and Portugal, as well as those of the Red Cross and the Vatican. This part of town looked like a world's fair exhibit and became known as the International Ghetto. Hundreds of people crowded into each house.

Raoul was relieved that the use of the Schutzpasses was saved. He knew this victory was the first step. Even so, many people were still disappearing each day.

20.

A Call for Help

The call came early one morning. Yellow star houses filled with unprotected Jews had been emptied of women and girls the night before. Trains weren't available, so Eichmann ordered them to march to their deaths. They had already left, trudging hundreds of miles toward the border where they would meet the trains that would take them the final miles to the death camps.

Raoul and Vilmos quickly put together supplies and joined trucks from the Red Cross speeding through town. They drove past a checkpoint into the now bombed-out Pest section of town. As they passed a crowd of Arrow Cross boys, the boys stepped back to reveal the body of an old man freshly shot through the head.

Such sights no longer shocked Raoul. But there was a sorrow that set his mouth into a grim line of determination. He leaned forward. "Faster, Vilmos. We must arrive before they start out again."

Finally they arrived at a crumbling building that had once been a brick factory. It was on the farthest edge of town. Now the place was crawling with soldiers carrying guns, their arms encircled with the hated red bands.

Raoul was out of the car before it stopped.

"Where is your commanding officer?" he demanded of

two privates. Vilmos opened his door calmly and strode after Raoul. The Red Cross cars behind them also parked. Two doctors and several nurses climbed out.

Raoul was standing face to face with a young officer. He waved official-looking Swedish and German papers in the man's face. Angry, the officer sputtered, "No! I have orders!"

In contrast, Raoul was demanding but calm. He spoke German. "Swedish Legation . . . Red Cross, orders directly from General Schmidthuber! Breaking international law!" Raoul kept talking. He wrote down the officer's name: Captain Weber. He threatened to report him to the German general at once. But if he helped, Raoul said he would recommend him for a promotion.

The officer faltered. He didn't know what kind of orders this man held in his hand, but he knew authority when he saw it. "All right," he hissed through his teeth. "But quickly! And no more than a hundred. I don't care how many passports—"

Raoul didn't wait to hear the end of the sentence. He rushed to the factory, the others following behind him.

"Captain Weber commands you to let us pass," he said to the guards at the door. The surprised young men stood aside as the Swede threw the bolt from the door and led his small band inside.

The stench was terrible. The smell of human waste and of bloody wounds combined with the smell of death. The windows were boarded up, and the room yawned like a huge black cave. It was eerily quiet.

Was anybody there? Anybody alive?

Raoul heard a low moaning. Doctors from the Red Cross turned on flashlights and aimed their beams into the room.

From where they stood, it seemed as if the floor was alive. Hundreds and hundreds of people were packed into the airless room.

Raoul raised a bullhorn and spoke into it with the same calm authority he'd used outside. "Attention! We have come for any of you with Swedish Schutzpasses! Any of you with such a pass, please raise your hand! You're to be taken back to Budapest!"

No one moved. They stared up with glazed eyes like mice trapped by the light. No one stirred. The women had been herded like animals and marched for hours. Then they'd been packed in here. The floor of the old building was rotting. People had fallen into holes, broken legs, been trampled. Some had been shot. There were no food, no toilets. The guards hadn't even hauled away people who had died. The survivors had been crammed together for eighteen hours, waiting to finish their brutal march to death.

Raoul knew this was the Germans' plan. If you can kill the spirit, it is much easier to kill the body.

"Listen to me," Raoul went on. "You now have food and toilets. There are doctors and nurses here to help those who need it the most. Look to those on either side of you. See if they need help."

There was some small movement, mostly at the mention of food. "Good," Raoul said. "Now, those of you with Swedish passes, come forward. It doesn't matter if you have them with you or not. It doesn't even matter if you asked for one and didn't get it yet. Your name is in the book. Stand up!"

Carrying flashlights, Raoul and some helpers hurried down the stairs into the teeming mob. They searched for the younger women in the group and helped them to their feet. Raoul made hasty notations in his book as he sent them forward. The Red Cross people took them up the stairs. More people were moving. More were coming alive. Raoul hoped it wasn't obvious to the guards that most people's names weren't in the book until they feverishly whispered them to him.

"Yes, you! Yes, I recognize you!" Raoul's firm voice could be heard as he sent more and more prisoners to the front of the factory. When the platform was filled with bruised, frightened women and girls, Red Cross workers hurried them outside to the first truck. Drivers had already unloaded medicine, food, and blankets, and they quickly replaced the load with precious human cargo. Another truck, then another were loaded.

Inside, the platform was full again. Raoul made his way through the room back toward the door. An old woman struggled to her feet and took his hand. He stopped, held her hand, and looked right at her. "I can't take any more, I'm sorry. I have to take the young ones first. I'm trying to save a nation."

The old woman squeezed his hand and let him go.

Up on the platform, Raoul said, "Out, all of you, hurry. Straight for the truck."

As the doors opened, one of the doctors took up the bullhorn. "Now! Look beside you. Is someone badly hurt? If so, raise your hand and call out. We'll come to you."

"Over here," someone called.

"Here, please help!" came another voice.

"A girl's injured here. She's bleeding!"

The nurses moved into the room.

And from the far corner, the words began to rise from

the crowd: "*Shema Yisrael, Adonai Eloheinu, Adonai Eḥad*—Hear, O Israel, the Lord is our God, the Lord is One." As voices joined in, the words of hope rippled through the crowd.

"Someone here needs help," an old woman called.

It was amazing. Ten minutes earlier, these people had been lifeless. Now they were helping their neighbors, reciting words of faith. It was as if a miracle had occurred. They were people again. Some of them were quietly removing the stars from their clothing. Many were already planning their escape.

Outside, Raoul and Vilmos got back into their car. They followed the last truck back to Budapest.

Back at the office, Raoul called his workers together. There were four hundred now, and many more were coming in all the time.

"Listen, everyone," he said. "This office is now open twenty-four hours a day. It is up to us to save thousands of people. You all know that Eichmann will stop at nothing. When he has no trains, he walks people to their deaths. Everyone, look at your feet. Men, take off your best shoes. Women, take off those pretty pumps. I want everyone in walking shoes. If you're caught and put on a march, walking shoes can save your life. I've seen too many people collapse and be shot because they're wearing the wrong shoes!"

There were now different parts of Section C. One was the humanitarian department, hundreds of people strong, which kept files on everyone who had an official pass. The section was run by Hugo Wohl. An "action" section called the Schutzling-Protocoll was responsible for saving lives.

It had secret meeting places and used many different uniforms to dress up like doctors or nurses, priests or nuns, even the Arrow Cross or Nazis.

Raoul himself only stopped in the office long enough to get messages and sign passes. He barely slept four hours a night. With so many lives to save, he couldn't afford to waste one minute.

21.

To the Rescue

In mid-November Raoul's driver Vilmos was arrested by the Arrow Cross. Two days later, Raoul hurried outside to meet his new driver, Sandor Ardai.

"Where would you like to go?" Sandor asked as Raoul got into the car.

"Arrow Cross headquarters. The first thing I need to do is get my old driver out of jail."

Sandor was stunned. This crazy man was going to march into Arrow Cross headquarters and demand they release a Jew? Just because he said so? Sandor had heard stories about Raoul Wallenberg, but this was outlandish. Yet he drove to headquarters and waited while Raoul bounded up the steps.

Fifteen minutes later, Raoul returned with a young man following behind him. "Sandor, this is Vilmos," Raoul said. "Let's get out of here."

Sandor didn't need to hear it twice. He stepped on the gas.

The note from Raoul read simply: "Meet me at the Jozsefvarosi railroad station. Come as early as you can. Bring your camera." Twenty-year-old Tom Veres felt his heart pounding as he rode the streetcar alone through the chilly morning air. He'd never been to the Jozsefvarosi station. It wasn't a polished passenger station in the middle of town. It was a freight station at the edge of Pest. In better days, farmers loaded cattle and grain there. Now there were no cattle or grain. The Nazis used it for other purposes.

When Tom arrived, he couldn't believe his eyes. The station was ringed by Hungarian Nazis and gendarmes, the Nazi-trained police from the countryside. And no wonder. Thousands of men were being loaded onto cattle cars. They had already been marched twenty miles to the railroad station and it was still early morning. Tom couldn't see the end of the line.

Tom saw Raoul already inside the ring of Nazis at a table with his large black ledger book open in front of him. His new Studebaker, with Vilmos at the wheel, was parked outside.

Tom couldn't believe it. Anyone with half a brain was trying to get out of the station. Wallenberg expected him to find a way in!

Tom summoned his courage and marched up to one of the gendarmes. Using the world's phoniest Swedish accent, he spoke in a mixture of broken Hungarian and German. "I'm a Swedish diplomat. I must go in to meet Raoul Wallenberg!"

The guard stared at him incredulously but didn't stop him as he marched past.

When Raoul saw Tom, he walked over to him and whispered, "Take as many pictures as you can."

Take pictures? Here? If he was caught, he'd be arrested at once, legation or no legation.

Tom kept his face blank while his mind raced to find a way to take the pictures. Calmly, he walked to Wallen-

At Jozsefvarosi station. Men form two lines to have their names checked at Wallenberg's table. They are guarded by Hungarian gendarmes. (Photography by Thomas Veres)

berg's car, got in the backseat, and closed the door. He took out the pocket knife he always carried and carefully cut a slit in his bulky scarf. He removed his camera from his pack, tried to guess at a good setting, and hid it in the folds of his scarf. Then he got back out and calmly walked through the train yard secretly snapping pictures.

Meanwhile, a man in an impressive uniform was looking over the books with Raoul. It was Laszlo Ferenczy, the head of the gendarmes, one of Raoul's informers. Ferenczy didn't want to be hanged as a war criminal. But he didn't want to be shot as a traitor to the Nazis either. His loyalty was good only as long as it didn't get him into trouble.

Raoul worked fast. "My people, get in line here," Raoul called. "All you need to do is to show me your pass!"

He walked to the line. "You, yes, I have your name

Taken from inside Wallenberg's car at the Jozsefvarosi railway station. Wallenberg, hands clasped behind him, stands at the table with the "Book of Life." Men form lines on either side. Cattle car in back at left; station in background, right. (Photography by Thomas Veres)

here. Where is your paper?" Raoul stood as the man fished around in his pockets, looking for a paper he never had. He pulled out his driver's license. "Fine. Next!"

Men caught on at once. They pulled out passports, eyeglass prescriptions, even deportation papers. Raoul and his assistants carefully wrote each name into the book. Tom knew that each man would get a file and a passport. The Nazis would have to answer for each one.

Tom moved along the line. He held his scarf at different angles, secretly taking pictures. While the gendarmes were stuffing men into cattle cars, Tom's camera recorded it all—the guns, the brutality, the human beings headed for death.

Tom Veres in the 1940s. (Courtesy of Thomas Veres)

A recent photograph of Tom Veres. (Courtesy of Thomas Veres)

"Tommy! Tommy!"

He froze at the sound of his name. If he was recognized, he'd be arrested and thrown on the train himself.

"Tommy! Here!"

In line, almost on the train was George Steiner, a good friend of Tom's since they'd been assigned seats next to each other in the first grade. Every year after that, they sat together by choice. George was so smart he was always first in the class. That could be annoying in a friend, but not in George.

Now the Germans were going to murder him.

Tom walked over to him, grabbed him by the collar, and said, "You dirty Jew, get over there!" He pointed George toward Wallenberg's line. "I said go! Are you deaf?" He kicked George's backside.

97

George caught on and slipped into the other line.

Raoul, who had pulled hundreds of men out of line, saw the Nazis getting angry. "Now, march back to Budapest, at once!" Raoul ordered.

As the men walked quickly toward the empty road leading home, Raoul turned toward the Nazis and started talking to them about health conditions, overcrowding on the trains, the dangers of breaking international law—anything to keep them from stopping his "Swedes."

Once the men had a good start, Raoul and Tom got into the car. On the drive back toward town, Tom found George. He took him to a safe house and took his picture for a protective Schutzpasse.

"Now stay here until your pass is ready," Tom warned his friend.

Tom now knew what it meant to be Raoul's "official" photographer.

The next day word came again that more Jews were being deported from the Jozsefvarosi station. Again, the station was surrounded by gendarmes with machine guns. They were loading thousands of men onto trains. Almost all of the soldiers were Hungarian Nazis. The only German officer there was a tall man with a hard face—Theodor Dannecker.

Again Raoul opened his book. Today Tom's Leica was already hidden in his scarf. Raoul started calling out common names that many men might answer to. Men began offering "papers," putting their names in the book, getting in line.

Then Tom saw his cousin Joseph. Gathering his nerve,

he marched over to him. "I know you have papers. Are you deaf? Get in line there."

Tom saw an actor, one of the biggest stars in Hungary. He went over and whispered to Raoul, who called out the man's name and dragged him off the train.

But what about the others? wondered Tom. Some of the men already on the train were waving their Schutzpasses. But they were trapped in the cars behind hundreds of others.

"All of you released by the Hungarian government, whose names I've already recorded, start marching back to town!" Raoul called out.

Three hundred released prisoners walked briskly back toward the city. It was then Tom saw his chance. He slipped under the train, inches from the armed guards. On the other side of the train, facing away from the station, he climbed onto the already filled car. The train had not yet been padlocked from this side. He jumped, pushing all his weight onto the bolt that held the door shut. The spring clicked. The long door slid back in its tracks.

Inside, the men, who a moment ago had stood prisoner in darkness, now blinked at the November sky. "Move, quick!" Tom hissed.

They poured off the back side of the train and formed a line at Wallenberg's table. They gave their names and headed for the road back toward the city.

In the station, the hubbub mounted until a voice—the only one as commanding as Wallenberg's—split the air: "NO MORE!"

Everyone turned. Hauptsturmführer Theodor Dannecker stalked from the background straight for Wallenberg. Dannecker was ruthless. He knew Raoul had no real power and was furious. The skull and crossbones nearly danced over the dark brim of his silver-gray hat. "This will stop!" he screamed.

A gendarme standing in front of Raoul immediately centered him in the sight of his automatic rifle.

Raoul closed his black book, turned calmly, and walked toward his car.

At the same time, a police officer noticed Tom on the train. He pointed his revolver at the young man. "You! Come here at once!"

Vilmos was already driving the Studebaker back toward town. Raoul opened the door and leaned out. "Tom! Jump!"

Tom didn't have a moment to think. He made the longest jump of his life.

Raoul pulled him inside and slammed the door as Vilmos stepped on the gas.

Raoul smiled at Tom. "Take a deep breath," he said. Then he looked back at the chaos at the train station. "I don't think we'll come back here for a while," he said.

One woman came to Raoul in the middle of the night. Her husband had been arrested. He had no papers. But Raoul was everyone's last chance. Raoul woke Vilmos, took his typewriter, and filled out a passport for the man as they drove to the railway station. It was still dark when they got there. He showed the guards the passport and called the man off the train. They drove back to town through empty streets.

Another night, a phone call awakened him. "They've taken my son and his wife and child from their beds, Mr. Wallenberg. All three of them had passes!"

Raoul called the private number of Peter Hain, the head of the Hungarian Gestapo. "You must let them go at once. We have all their papers. Must I come and get them myself?"

Hain promised they would be released. Raoul went back to bed.

When they didn't come home, Raoul continued to press for the reason. Hain finally told him the truth: the family had been released as promised. However, on their way home, they'd been found by a gang of Arrow Cross. The thugs tortured them for ten days, then threw them into the icy Danube River. Only the wife lived till morning. A boatman fished her out.

Only two days after Tom went with Raoul to the train station, George Steiner's mother came to the Ulloi Street offices looking for Tom. He could see that she was very upset.

"What is it?" Tom asked. "What's wrong?"

"They've taken George away. You've got to help me!"

"They took him from the safe house?" Tom asked.

"No. He found out that his fiancée was in another house just two corners away. He couldn't wait to see her . . . it was just down the street. But two Arrow Cross thugs caught him."

"Arrow Cross?" asked Tom, and his heart sank. He knew the Arrow Cross felt free to do anything they wanted with Jews who had no papers. Anything. There was no way to find out which two thugs were responsible, or what might have happened to George.

Why couldn't he have waited for his papers?

"Tommy, please do something!"

101

The boy turned to his best friend's mother. "It's impossible," he said. "There's nothing we can do."

Sadly, he walked back into the office. Tom knew George had been murdered. He never saw his friend again.

22.

The Noose Tightens

Colonel Adolph Eichmann was furious. Every time he turned around, that Swede was in his way. Two thousand people saved from marches. Fifteen thousand men taken from labor camps. Who did he think he was?

"I'm going to kill that Jew-dog Wallenberg!" yelled Eichmann, ignoring the people surrounding him and the Swedish Red Cross worker nearby.

The Red Cross worker reported Eichmann's threat to Minister Danielsson, who reported it to Stockholm. The diplomats in Stockholm complained to the Nazi Foreign Ministry in Berlin.

"Surely the colonel was joking," said the Nazi minister. "Besides, your Wallenberg's work is bothersome, not to mention illegal."

The official in Berlin telegrammed Budapest. Hitler's proconsul, Edmund Veesenmayer, went to talk to Eichmann. "Never speak so carelessly again. If you have Wallenberg killed, it must not look like we are involved."

The Allies—the Americans, the British, and the Soviets—had captured most of Hungary. Now they were coming for Budapest. Bombs fell day and night. Large guns boomed from the ground. The city was surrounded on three sides. Everyone fled but the Jews, who had been put into the Central Ghetto.

The ghetto was sealed off. No one could get in or out. There was hardly enough food to keep anyone alive. There was no medicine, and no heating fuel was left to ward off the deep December cold.

Raoul knew that there was little time. Certainly, Eichmann had planned a "final solution" for the Jews of Budapest. Locking so many people into the Central Ghetto was part of the plan. If the Germans locked them all in one place, Raoul knew Eichmann could kill them much more quickly.

He couldn't let that happen.

The situation was only slightly better in the Swedish-protected houses. Thirteen-year-old Tommy Lapid and his mother lived in a bedroom crowded with twenty other people. His father was already dead. At night, when the lights were off, Tommy and his mother lay awake listening to the gunshots that peppered the night. They knew the shots came from the Danube River just blocks away.

In the darkness, Tommy said, "I'm so hungry. If only we could share one piece of bread."

Tommy's mother felt her heart tear. What kind of mother can't give her child one piece of bread?

The next morning, a fierce pounding came from downstairs. Below, the front door slammed open, and they could hear angry Hungarian voices. "Every able-bodied woman is to come with us!"

Tommy and his mother looked at each other in terror. Downstairs they heard the guard arguing unsuccessfully with the soldiers. Finally, gendarmes with machine guns ran from room to room, pulling out all the women and girls.

Tommy hugged his mother as hard as he could. They were both crying. "Good-bye, my son," she whispered.

"Good-bye," he said. The soldiers burst into their room, and they both knew they would never see each other again.

And then she was gone. Tommy was an orphan.

Two hours later, the door to the bedroom opened again. His mother and the other women rushed in. Tommy couldn't believe his eyes. Was it a dream or a miracle? As his mother hugged and kissed him, she repeated only one word: "Wallenberg."

Raoul strode out of the Foreign Ministry after one more meeting of another round of threats and another round of promises.

As he came to the front door, it swung open. There, surrounded by soldiers, stood Adolph Eichmann.

The two men studied each other. Raoul smiled.

"Why, Herr Eichmann. An unexpected pleasure."

"Yes, Mr. Wallenberg. Unexpected, indeed."

"I'd been hoping to run into you."

"Oh?" the colonel asked. "And why was that?"

"Why, to invite you to dinner. Next Friday perhaps? Your deputy, Mr. Krumey, is welcome as well."

"Friday would be fine. Seven-thirty? At your apartment?"

"Yes. Would you like directions?"

Eichmann now smiled as well. "Oh, I'm sure I can find my way."

Raoul's last stop of the day was at the offices on Tigris Street. Even though it was near midnight, he had to leave instructions for the next day. He had never felt so tired. But he was able to work well on only four hours of sleep a night. As he left his office, he looked around at the floors covered with sleeping people. There was so much to be done.

"Mr. Wallenberg?" A man's voice came from behind him. "I don't know what to do. It's my wife, Agnes."

He turned to find Tibor Vandor, a young Hungarian who worked in Section C.

"Your wife? Who took her? How long ago?"

"No, no. She's having a baby. No hospital will let her in. And we can't find a doctor."

Raoul almost smiled. "Well, where is she, man? Get her down to my car quickly while I call a doctor."

Raoul and Vilmos picked up the doctor on the ride to Raoul's apartment. When they arrived, Raoul led the young couple inside and helped Agnes into bed. Then he placed a pillow on the floor of the unheated hall and lay down to get some sleep.

In the small hours of the morning, the doctor shook him awake. "Mr. Wallenberg! This time I'm waking you with good news. You're the godfather of a beautiful little girl."

The diplomatic pouch was leaving for Sweden. Raoul wanted to make sure a letter to his mother went with it.

Dearest Mother,
I feel bad not to write more often, but
again all you'll get is a hurried letter in the
diplomatic pouch. The situation here is
dangerous and exciting but I'm snowed un-
der with work. There are bandits roaming
the city. . . . We hear the cannons of the ap-
proaching Russians night and day. . . . I'm
almost single-handedly representing our le-
gation at the government offices. I've met
about ten times with the foreign minister,
twice with the prime minister, etc. I was
good friends with the wife of the foreign
minister. She has now left for Italy. There
is a great food shortage in Budapest. But
we laid in a good supply in advance. . . . I
really thought I'd be with you for Christ-
mas. But I must send you my Christmas
greetings, and at the same time, my good
wishes for the New Year. I hope the longed-
for peace will soon be here! . . . I send
kisses to the entire family.

When the secretary had finished typing it up, Raoul added, "Love to Nina and her little girl!"

Raoul sighed. When would he see his beautiful mother again? Or meet his first little niece? It seemed like twenty years ago that he'd seen Nina in Berlin, but it was less than six months.

Another day, another crisis. "Mr. Wallen-berg!" The young man panted for breath. "I've been sent from the orphanage. They just brought us dozens of children whose parents are being marched away right now."

"Do you have the children's names?" Raoul's mind was working quickly. He took the offered list.

"Hugo. Quickly! Have Schutzpasses typed up bearing all these last names. Leave the first names blank. Vilmos! Get the car. We must find the parents and make sure these children don't become orphans, after all."

Raoul sighed and stretched out his legs in the back of the car. It never stopped, never let up, not for one second. This was one night he was glad to be going home. Maybe he could get one extra hour's sleep. Edith Wohl would call only in case of an extreme emergency. Maybe he could even finish his supper before the telephone rang again.

The car stopped in front of his apartment. Raoul walked quickly up the stairs. Just as he opened the door, he heard another car drive up and turned around.

It was a long, shiny black car with red and black Nazi flags displayed on the front fender. The chauffeur opened the back door. Adolph Eichmann and Deputy Krumey stepped out.

It was Friday.

They had come for dinner.

23.

Dinner

Raoul let himself into his apartment. There was hardly any food in the kitchen—certainly not enough for a dinner party. There wasn't time to cook the food even if he had it. He had to think quickly. Then he remembered Lars Berg complaining about his cook. Lars, also a secretary at the legation, rented a villa from a family who'd fled Budapest. The villa came with a cook. Lars had complained because she knew only how to make large, fancy meals.

Raoul called quickly. Thank goodness Lars was home. He invited Raoul and his guests over immediately.

By the time they arrived at Berg's villa, the table was set with the finest crystal and china. The two diplomats, Lars Berg and Gotte Carlsson, were dressed for dinner and Lars was mixing drinks. It seemed as if this party had been well planned for days!

Eichmann and Krumey wore their best SS uniforms. From the beginning they sat straight, suspecting their host, prepared to leap out of their seats at the first sign of danger.

Somehow the discomfort of his guests put Raoul at ease. Adolph Eichmann was sitting in Lars's living room. Close up, he didn't have super powers. He wasn't a monster, only a man. But he was the one man who could call off the final massacre of the ghetto. Raoul doubted anything could change Eichmann's mind. Still he had to try.

Adolph Eichmann was used to making people afraid. He snapped his fingers and a thousand soldiers stood at attention. He spoke a word and ten thousand people died. He knew Wallenberg was determined to save the very people whom he was determined to kill. But instead of bargaining with him or begging him, here was this under secretary of a neutral nation chatting as if they were on a pleasure cruise.

"Gentlemen, dinner is served," said Lars.

In good spirits, the three Swedes led the way to the table, with the two Germans following. The cook prepared an outstanding meal. They were served elegant food and fine wine. And their conversation was so pleasant that Raoul noticed his guest starting to relax.

After dinner, the men returned to the living room for coffee. When they were seated, Raoul turned off all the lights, strode over to the picture window, and opened the drapes.

The effect was stunning. The sky was bright with red and gold. It looked like fireworks. But it was the fire from thousands of Russian cannons and guns as they closed in on Budapest.

"The war is almost over, gentlemen. Wouldn't you say?" he asked. "How long before Budapest falls? Weeks? Days?"

"Don't be so hasty," said Eichmann calmly. "Budapest will be held as though it were Berlin."

"Ah, yes. But how long will Berlin be held?"

"The führer has not yet unleashed his secret weapons. The tide will turn. You'll see."

"The Nazis never had Russia. Now you've lost France and Romania. Yugoslavia is gone. The countries of the Third Reich are falling like dominos. Even you must admit the war is lost. The Russians are almost here. Why not leave town while you can? There's no way you're ever going to wipe out a whole race. In fact, it seems clear that Hitler's plans to conquer the world were doomed from the start," Raoul continued.

Adolph Eichmann sat looking at Raoul. He was unable to hide his amazement. How could this fool sit in a Nazi-run city, in a room with an SS colonel, and calmly insult the führer?

One by one, Raoul questioned Adolph Hitler's beliefs. Colonel Eichmann gave the Nazi answer to each question. Then Raoul responded to his answer. It became clear to the other men in the room that the Nazi's rote answers sounded hollow next to Raoul's well-reasoned arguments.

Finally, Eichmann said, "I admit that you're right, Herr Wallenberg. I never really believed in Nazism. But look at what it's given me: power and wealth. I know this pleasant life of mine will soon be over. Planes will no longer bring me women and wine from Paris or food from the Orient. My horses, my dogs, my luxurious villa here in Budapest will soon be taken over by the Russians. I myself will be shot on the spot.

"There's no escape for me. But if I obey my orders from Berlin, if I use my powers harshly enough, I may still have some time to enjoy life here in Budapest." Then Adolph Eichmann paused, staring at Raoul Wallenberg as if the two of them were alone in the room. "I warn you, Mr. Legation Secretary. I will do my best to stop you. Your diplomat's passport won't help you if I find it necessary to have you

. . . removed. Accidents do happen. Even to a 'neutral' diplomat."

With those words, he stood up. Neither he nor Raoul had shown any anger during the evening. Eichmann did not display any now.

"A very pleasant good night to you, Mr. Wallenberg. And to my hosts, thank you for a particularly pleasant evening."

Everyone shook hands at the door, and the two Germans disappeared into their limousine.

Raoul was stunned. How could someone murder old men, young men, pretty girls, grandmothers, little children, and babies for no other reason than because he enjoyed horses and foreign food? Raoul knew that he hadn't changed Eichmann's thinking. He also knew the most dangerous enemy was a cornered enemy. And Adolph Eichmann was quickly becoming a cornered man.

24.

A Farewell Visit

Raoul knew his life was in danger. He kept on the move, somehow turning up where he was needed. Every night he slept in a different place. He carried his belongings in the knapsack he'd brought to Budapest.

Raoul was grateful for his driver, Vilmos Langfelder. The two were about the same age. Villy had been an engineer before the war. He was quiet yet had a sense of humor like Raoul's. Most important, he had nerves of steel. Raoul had saved Villy twice, once from the labor camp, then from the hands of the Arrow Cross. In return, Vilmos came to Raoul's aid more than once. The two men trusted each other completely.

Two nights after the dinner with Eichmann, a large truck rammed Raoul's car, leaving it badly damaged, and sped off into the December darkness. Somehow Raoul and Vilmos got out of the car, bruised and shaken.

As soon as he made certain Vilmos was all right, Raoul marched off at a quick clip.

"Where are you going?" Vilmos asked.

"To Eichmann's headquarters at the Majestic Hotel."

"Are you crazy? He just tried to kill us."

"I think that merits a protest, don't you?"

At SS headquarters, Adolph Eichmann pretended to be

People being marched from yellow star houses to the ghetto along Baross Utza, overseen by the regular Hungarian police. Note: *The woman in the foreground is hiding her yellow star. As the policeman focuses his attention elsewhere, the woman makes her escape. In fact, according to Veres, she was successful.* (Photography by Thomas Veres)

surprised and sympathetic. But as Raoul left, the colonel said, "Don't worry. I'll try again."

Besides his fight with Raoul, Eichmann still had two important tasks to finish before he left Budapest. One was to force the thousands of Jews in the "protected houses" into the Central Ghetto. There they could all be killed at once. The other was to personally make sure that every member of the Jewish Council was dead.

One evening before Christmas, Eichmann was in his office at the Majestic Hotel when news came that the Russians were closing in on the city.

Despite the remarks that he'd shared with Raoul at dinner, the colonel didn't want to die for the Nazis. He had to leave Budapest soon. Before his departure, he would have to give the order to kill the seventy thousand people in the ghetto. But there was one thing he'd take great pleasure in doing himself.

A few minutes later the telephone rang at the porter's lodge inside the ghetto. When Jakob Takacs answered it, a German voice said, "All the members of the Jewish Council must be at the council headquarters at nine o'clock. Colonel Eichmann's orders!"

Wallenberg, however, had obtained secret reports warning that the men on the council were in danger. Instead of going to the council room, they all hid.

At exactly 9:00 P.M., three carloads of armed SS men pulled up to the ghetto. Eichmann and two other officers got out of the middle car and stalked into the council room. It was empty.

Angrily, they went to the porter's lodge and banged on the door. "The Jewish Council members! Where are they?"

Jakob looked puzzled and scared. "I was told to have them here at nine o'clock tomorrow morning!"

Eichmann flew into a rage and started yelling in German. Jakob Takacs said, "I'm sorry, Colonel. I don't understand German very well. Perhaps I misunderstood."

As Eichmann was screaming, Jakob's sister came running out of their room to see what was wrong.

"Don't just stand there, you piece of garbage, get them here right now. Now! If they're not rounded up in five minutes, I'll shoot you—and your sister."

"I can't, sir. I told them tomorrow morning. Who knows where they are now? There are seventy thousand people packed into two hundred and seventy-five houses. Who can find anybody at this time of night?"

In response, one of Eichmann's aides cracked the porter over the head with his pistol. He hit him again and again until Jakob fell bleeding to the floor.

The Nazi turned to his sister. "When your brother wakes up, tell him that if every single member of the council is not here at nine o'clock tomorrow morning, I give my word that both you and your brother will be shot dead on the spot."

The next morning, the council members gathered before nine o'clock. They knew by coming they faced certain death. But if they didn't turn themselves in, how many other people would die? Together they waited. Two hours passed.

Finally, a report came. Only one road remained open leading out of Budapest. Adolph Eichmann and all of his SS officers had taken it out of the city during the night.

25.

Merry Christmas

It was the night of Christmas Eve. Sitting in his car as he drove through the dark streets of Budapest, Raoul couldn't help but remember the years gone by. In Sweden, Christmas Eve is celebrated with as much gusto as Christmas Day. Families gather for a lavish smorgasbord before opening their presents. Then, at midnight, the entire family goes to a candlelight service. He smiled at the memory of how happily his little sister, Nina, had celebrated Christmas when she was a girl. Would there soon come a time when he could see Nina's daughter dance with the same joy? Perhaps someday he'd even see the same happiness in a little girl of his own.

Christmas. Hanukkah. Children should be singing, laughing, dancing. On this evening, though, five thousand Jewish children were crowded into orphanages, their parents missing or dead. Since the beginning of December, the Nazi government had packed these children into the Central Ghetto, where many of them were dying of hunger and cold even before the Germans launched the pogrom intended to kill them all.

Raoul had done everything possible to save the children. That very day he'd organized a joint appeal by the ministers of the neutral nations to protest the harsh treatment of the children. But even such a plea might not do much good. Since the Hungarian Nazi government had moved out of town, no one was left to run Budapest except the Arrow Cross. It was hard for Raoul to believe that, because of their belief in Hitler's cause, the Arrow Cross tortured and killed people. It seemed more likely they killed because they enjoyed it. Raoul sighed. Who could enjoy shooting shivering, defenseless children?

Raoul had spent the last few days saving one group of children being marched to their deaths inside the ghetto. He also stopped a cartload of thirty infants and toddlers who were being taken by the Arrow Cross to be killed in the Danube. The strong letter of protest he'd written to the Hungarian government might not do much good. But perhaps it would keep the children safe for two or three days. By then, the Russians might have taken Budapest, and the Arrow Cross might be gone.

No one was safe anymore. Earlier, the Arrow Cross had raided the main Swedish Legation in Buda. Someone there had called the office on Ulloi Street in time to warn the workers to scatter. It seemed the Arrow Cross had been looking for Raoul. They released the rest of the Swedish diplomats.

Raoul was now a hunted man. He instructed his driver, Vilmos, to drop him off on a dark side street. Slipping through the night to the secret apartment on Uri Street, where Per Anger and Lars Berg were hiding, he spent Christmas Eve with his friends sleeping with furniture pushed against the door, their pistols within easy reach.

The next day, Raoul and Per went to share Christmas dinner with most of the representatives of the Swedish Legation at the home of their friends Elizabeth and Alexander Kasser, from the Red Cross. Mrs. Kasser knew they'd all been working hard and in great danger for a long time. They needed some cheering up. The week before, she went to the countryside to get her two children, four-year-old Michael and two-year-old Mary. She thought it would be safer for the family to be together when the Russians arrived. When she brought the children back from the country, she smuggled in some beef and a milk cow now hidden in the garage.

Their Christmas dinner was jolly. The Russians had closed the ring around the city during the night. Surely the end was in sight. At the table, the Swedish diplomats and the Red Cross workers all talked about what they would do after the war.

Raoul happily joined in. He had been thinking about his own plans. He wanted to stay in Budapest to start the difficult work of helping families rebuild their lives after the war. Many had lost everything they owned.

Raoul stayed with the Kassers after the others left. He thanked them again for the wonderful gift they'd given him: a valuable sculpture of Athena, the Greek goddess of wisdom and beauty. As an architect, he loved the lines of the sculpture. It made him hopeful of living again in a world touched by beauty, not bombs.

Raoul loved the family atmosphere at the Kassers' home. He played with little Michael and Mary and told the Kassers how much he missed being with his own family, especially on Christmas. "I hope we'll never again have to live through times like these," he told the children.

That was the prayer in each of their hearts.

The next day reports reached Raoul at the Swedish Legation that the Nazi janitor of an orphanage on Munkacsi Mihaly Street had kept food from reaching the children for two days. On Christmas Day, he had falsely reported that some of the children had escaped. At 4:00 P.M., the Arrow Cross came and lined up all of the children in the courtyard. Starving and dressed in rags, the children waited as the Arrow Cross counted them twice to make certain none were missing.

An hour later, the janitor called the Arrow Cross again. This time the soldiers forced the terrified, freezing children to stand in the bitterly cold courtyard for more than an hour. They shot two of the older children dead. Then the Arrow Cross soldiers lined up the other children, the orphanage director, and his wife and marched them through the winter streets, arguing over which part of the icy Danube River to throw the huddled youngsters into.

When they reached the river, the sky suddenly filled with Allied planes. Bombs started falling all around them. "Run for your lives!" the Arrow Cross shouted to each other. The frantic children ran, too.

When the air raid was over, the furious soldiers went from house to house. They found only five children and one teacher. Those six were shot dead.

Meanwhile, across town, more Arrow Cross soldiers raided another shelter. This one was on Vilma Kiralyno Street. Two old women, the children in the sickroom, and two teenagers were killed. When a nurse asked permission to bundle up the children who were to be taken away, she was killed, too.

Raoul didn't know how much more of this any of them could stand. He put down the report.

"Merry Christmas," he whispered.

Not long after he finished the report, Raoul's phone rang. Eight Arrow Cross thugs had just raided a house full of old people, women, and babies. Not just any house but a Swedish protected house on Katona Josef Street. Angrily, Raoul called the Foreign Ministry office.

"How can you do this?" he asked. "This house is protected by the government—your government!"

"Yes, yes, Mr. Wallenberg. A mistake, I'm sure. Your 'Swedes' will be returned."

Raoul didn't trust this answer. He ran for his car and took Tom Veres along as his interpreter. When they arrived at the Swedish house, the front door was standing wide open. Raoul strode in, Tom just a few steps behind him. It was dead quiet. The house was empty. The only person there was a captain from a division of the Arrow Cross checking to make sure no one was hiding.

"Ask him where my people are," Raoul said.

Tom asked, and the man said, "What people?"

"The people who live in the house."

The soldier sneered. "They're in the Danube."

Raoul said, "Ask him why."

Tom asked why.

"Because they were rotten Jews," the soldier said.

That was the end of it. This time, Raoul was too late.

26.

Showdown

There was only a week between Christmas and New Year's, yet those last dark days of December seemed to stretch on and on. Bombs and gunfire were heard all the time. The Russian army was so close the soldiers were visible. Even so, the German SS and the Hungarian Arrow Cross still ran Budapest.

Raoul knew it was a race against time to keep alive the seventy thousand Jews in the ghetto and the thirty thousand in protected houses. Every hour that people remained alive was one hour closer to freedom. But each hour was hard won.

General Schmidthuber, the highest ranking Nazi left in town, had orders to hold Budapest until the last German soldier was dead and to kill all the Jews before the Russians came. The Germans were still well organized and worked with deadly efficiency.

The Arrow Cross and its death squads, although hardly organized, killed anybody they caught—Gentile or Jew. If an Arrow Cross thug found someone on the street, his victim's fate depended on his mood. Most of the time it meant certain death. But would he shoot the person on the spot, take him to the river, or bring him to Arrow Cross headquarters to be tortured first?

So, while the Germans made organized plans to kill everyone in the ghetto and the protected houses, the Arrow Cross raided houses and marched hundreds of people to their deaths.

Meanwhile, the "legation" offices on Ulloi Street kept expanding. Every time the owners of another office fled the large building, Raoul took over the space. Hundreds of Swedish "employees" now lived at the legation. The offices, the hallways, even the stairs were teeming with people. Most of them were still working. One section made new files and filled out new passes. Another section still sent people and food out on rescue missions. The phone rang continuously. Almost everyone had candles because the lights were constantly flickering on and off.

Raoul knew that he needed new help in high places to stop the Germans and the Arrow Cross. As if in answer to his prayers, the help arrived one bitterly cold day. Between missions around the city, Raoul came to the office to sign new passes. He was in his office working by candlelight when a man in a leather coat found his way through the legation to Raoul's office. He told Wallenberg he was a messenger from Pal Szalai, a high officer of the Arrow Cross. Pal Szalai, he said, wanted to help save Jews.

Wallenberg thought fast. "If it's true, if he's willing and has influence, have him see that the officials who are still missing from the raid on our Buda legation are freed."

The next night, to everyone's amazement, the Swedish officials returned. Raoul phoned the "leather coat man," Karoly Szabo, at once. "Please invite Mr. Szalai to join me for dinner," he said.

The Arrow Cross officer arrived at the legation the next night in a thick winter coat. With him were two bodyguards. Raoul offered his hand. "Mr. Szalai."

"Mr. Wallenberg."

"Do come upstairs where we can talk privately."

The legation was blacked out but protected Jews stood on each side of the stairs holding candles. They knew about Pal Szalai, and few could hide their curiosity.

Raoul and Pal entered the private office. The bodyguards waited outside. "May I offer you some dinner?"

"Thank you, no. You know why I'm here. I'm Arrow Cross, but I'm with them in name only. I've come to offer my services."

Raoul studied him, trying to read behind his eyes. He had developed a sixth sense about people, often needing to decide in an instant who was telling the truth. He thought Pal Szalai was telling the truth.

"Why the change of heart, Mr. Szalai?"

"I've lost the stomach for murder. The Arrow Cross used to be a political party. Now it's the lowest kind of animal behavior. I've had enough. A strange thing, yes? An Arrow Cross officer who discovers he has a heart? I'll help you however I can. That's the best way to prove I'm sincere.

"I'll start right now. Your life is in danger this very minute, Mr. Wallenberg. Yes, I know that you've marched into hell to threaten the devil himself. But the next time you march into hell, SS or Arrow Cross, you won't be coming out. You need to go into hiding at once."

Raoul smiled. "Thanks for the concern, Szalai. But I have to give myself as freely as I give my signature." He motioned to the passes, newly signed, on his desk.

"As you wish. At least let me suggest a safe apartment and give you bodyguards. You're no good to anyone if you're dead."

"All right. I accept. If you're as good as your word, Mr. Szalai, we could become very good friends."

124

"I think we might, Mr. Wallenberg."

"We mustn't risk being seen together very often. Shall we continue to use Karoly Szabo?" Raoul asked.

Pal Szalai smiled. "He can still move around freely. He'll make a good go-between."

The two men shook hands, and the Arrow Cross officer disappeared into the night. Two armed Arrow Cross men, now Raoul's bodyguards, stayed behind.

Pal Szalai was as good as his word. From him, Raoul kept track of the comings and goings of the Arrow Cross and the SS. He protected Raoul on New Year's Eve, when the Swiss Legation was raided. Tragically, several men and women with whom Raoul worked closely were killed.

On New Year's Day, Raoul got word that a Swedish house on Revai Street was being raided. Raoul arrived with an armed guard provided by Szalai in time to save all eighty people who were being taken to their deaths.

Raoul still had some secret stashes of money and food to use as bribes. He used them both the first week in January.

He used the cash to make a deal with Szalai to place one hundred armed guards on the walls that encircled the Central Ghetto. They had orders to shoot anyone who tried to enter the ghetto by force. No more random raids by the Arrow Cross.

As Raoul stood outside the ghetto, watching the guards take their places, he moved quietly over to where Pal Szalai was giving orders. "This is my diplomatic career's greatest achievement," he said in a quiet voice.

But Wallenberg had no time to celebrate. He'd received an order from the Szalasi government that all "interna-

tional" Jews—those in Swedish, Swiss, Red Cross, and Por-
tuguese houses—were to be moved into the Central Ghetto
at once.

Raoul wrote a strong letter of protest. The people in the
ghetto were already starving to death, he said. There can
be no good reason to add thirty-five thousand more.

The next day, however, Dr. Erno Vajna, the new Hungarian minister of the interior, ordered everyone in the
protected houses to be ready to move on an hour's notice.

Raoul had to delay the plan. He knew the Arrow Cross
needed food badly. On January 4, he went in person to make
a deal with the Arrow Cross. It was like a card game with
Jewish lives for stakes. Both sides knew the Russians would
capture Budapest within days. The SS and the Arrow Cross
had only days to move all the Jews into the ghetto and kill
them. Raoul had only days to keep them alive until the
war ended.

"You need food, I've got it," he said. "Keep your hands
off the people in the safe houses and I'll give you food."

The Arrow Cross agreed. Raoul wrote out a long memo
putting the deal in writing.

The next day without warning five thousand Swedish
Jews were forced to move into the ghetto. Raoul, angry, set
up a meeting immediately with the leaders of the Arrow
Cross. He found the leaders in the basement of the Arrow
Cross building sitting around a table by candlelight. Dr.
Vajna was there, as was Pal Szalai.

"You take my people, you get no food," Raoul said.

"You'd be doing yourself a favor if you moved into a
cellar yourself, instead of risking your neck for a bunch of
Jews," said an Arrow Cross man with ties to the SS.

Raoul stood up slowly. "There is no point in trying to

deal with someone who holds those views," he said. He turned around and walked out.

The men sat staring after him. The same man turned toward Dr. Vajna. "We've got to deal with him on very short order," he said.

The meeting broke up. Szalai sent word to Raoul. "Get out of sight. Now!"

Raoul breathed a long sigh and turned over the last Schutzpasse in the pile. Young Tom Veres stood nearby, looking over the pictures he'd taken for the passes. When would this all end? The Allies were taking so long . . .

"Enough for the day, Tom," he said. "Let's go see where the Russians are." He sounded almost lighthearted, as if he'd suggested they go on a picnic.

Tom smiled in return. In the midst of chaos, it was easy to feel hopeful with Raoul. Surely the worst was almost over. Soon Tom could stop living at the Ulloi Street offices and return to his parents' apartment near the river. Soon his mother, Berta, would be cooking some of her bountiful meals, and his photographer father, Paul, could take pictures of carefree people, happy times. With each passing day that hope was closer to becoming reality. Tom said, "Let me call my friend. I'd bet he'd like to go."

Within minutes, Raoul, Tom, Tom's friend, and Vilmos met at the car. Raoul and Tom got in first and sat in the middle of the backseat. Three large gendarmes on Raoul's payroll sat on either side of them next to the windows. As the car dodged through Budapest's war-torn streets, Raoul and Tom were wedged together in the crowded backseat.

"This reminds me of the time I was kidnapped by bandits on my way back to school in Michigan," Raoul said, smiling as the car rumbled across the bridge to Buda. German guards gazed in at them but waved the car on when they saw the uniformed soldiers in the backseat. The car wound its way up Castle Hill and stopped at the top, where large German guns blasted away at the Russians just across the river. The men in the car piled out and stood looking at the red fire of shells exploding in the sky.

"How long till they get here, do you think?" Raoul asked Tom. Neither Raoul nor his young friend was happy about the Russians taking over Budapest. But it had to be better than these days of horror and death that went on and on.

"Let's take some pictures," Raoul said gamely. Tom had brought his Leica as well as an eight-millimeter movie camera. They posed by the guns and cannons as blithely as if they were on a school outing.

Finally, when Russian gunfire started hitting only yards from where they stood, they got back into the car. As they passed checkpoints heading back to Pest, Tom commented on their different license plates—diplomatic, Red Cross, Hungarian. "We should have a button to press to change the plates automatically," he joked.

Raoul laughed heartily, hoping the worst was over, not knowing the worst was yet to come.

27.

Pogrom

Snow swirled through the city on Monday, January 8. The call from Jokai Street came too late. One hundred eighty children, women, and men were taken from the Swedish house at gunpoint and marched through slush-covered streets to Arrow Cross headquarters on Varoshaz Street, where they were tortured. Then they were marched to the Danube and shot dead.

Raoul collected as much money and food as possible and gave it to Pal Szalai, who used it to pay armed guards to stand guard in front of each Swedish house. This gave Raoul comfort, but he couldn't forget the one hundred eighty Jews for whom the guards arrived too late.

The terrors of that snowy day weren't over. After nightfall, a band of heavily armed Arrow Cross thugs converged on the Ulloi Street offices. Inside, the employees of Section C awoke to angry pounding on the door. The Arrow Cross burst into the darkened offices, shining flashlights into the faces of the many frightened people who stayed there. They didn't know Edith Wohl was upstairs, placing an emergency telephone call.

"Everyone line up!" the Arrow Cross officer demanded

in Hungarian. "Hurry! Faster! Or we'll shoot you on the spot."

Tom Veres's heart was pounding as he was forced into line. It was finally happening. This is how it felt to be in the line from which he had so often helped save people about to be marched to death. This is how it felt to know that only a matter of minutes stood between help arriving in time or too late.

"All of you, down the stairs, quietly! One word and you're dead."

The Arrow Cross took special delight in stealing the Swede's own workers right out of his offices. Maybe they hadn't found him, but they'd shown him who was boss.

Together the people of Section C, who had worked so long and hard to save others, marched through the eerily quiet streets of Budapest. Their footfalls were muffled by the layer of snow that was quickly turning black. They were herded into the district Arrow Cross headquarters. Very few Jews who saw the inside of this place ever lived to give a description. They were forced to face the walls, their hands above their heads. "Please," one mother begged in Hungarian. "We're not Jewish."

Laughing, the soldier took her daughter. "Okay. If you're Christian, let's hear the 'Our Father.'"

The girl was so terrified she couldn't speak.

Laughing, the soldiers beat up both mother and daughter.

Tom Veres was standing next to a short fellow who always asked questions. "Do you know which way the Danube is?" he whispered.

"When you hear shooting, you'll know we're there," Tom replied.

"Everybody back in line. It's time for a little walk to the river," growled one guard. He turned to a couple of soldiers sitting nearby. "It's your turn to take them to the Danube," he said.

"Are you crazy? There's a blizzard out there. We just got back from taking the last group. Look, our boots aren't dry yet."

"In line, I say. Now!"

Wearily, the co-workers assembled into line. It was then the door burst open.

"What are you doing? Don't you know these are Swedes? All of your food is coming from Swedes. You've made a very serious mistake. You'd better let them go."

Together the people of Section C all turned. A truckload of Budapest policemen were filling the room, their guns drawn.

Raoul Wallenberg stared at the officer. "You heard me. Let them go. Now!"

The Arrow Cross captain looked angrily at the machine guns surrounding him. He glared back at the Swede. A moment later, the captain released his prisoners.

Elizabeth Kasser, Raoul's friend from the Red Cross, found him in a makeshift office in a cellar of Ulloi Street.

"The Arrow Cross have taken my husband, Alexander," she said.

Raoul's face looked drawn. "Well, the good news is this. I just heard an announcement on the radio. An all-out search is on for me and your husband. They wouldn't need to search for him if they still had him, would they? Knowing Alexander, I'm sure he's escaped."

131

They talked for a few minutes. Raoul told her sadly about the raid on the Swedish house on Jokai Street.

Later, Elizabeth found out Raoul was right. Her husband had escaped from the Arrow Cross. The whole family hid until after the war.

Raoul, with Vilmos and the Wohls, had found a secret hiding place in which to live: the vault of the Hazai Bank, near the ghetto. "Have you ever seen a bank vault that held greater treasure than this one?" he asked Pal Szalai when he came to visit. "Human lives, not money."

Raoul had maps on which he carefully plotted the Russian advance with pins and drawings. In November, he had set up a new part of Section C headed by a brilliant economist, Rezso Muller. They were putting together a plan to rebuild the homes—and lives—of the Jews of Hungary. As soon as the Soviets "liberated" Budapest, they would start by feeding and clothing the thousands of people near death.

When he had the time, Raoul visited Muller to see how the plans were coming. He told Rezso he wanted to meet with the Russians as soon as possible, so that the new Wallenberg Institute of Reconstruction could begin work. There was so much to be done.

The call reached Tom Veres at the legation offices on Ulloi Street, where he was waiting out the few days until the war was over.

The superintendent of the Gerbeaud Palace, the apartment building where Tom's family lived, was on the other end.

"Tom, your parents were taken away! They've all been taken!"

A feeling of dread lodged in Tom's stomach. He pleaded

with the man to slow down and to explain exactly what had happened. Everyone from the block-long building had taken refuge in the cellar because of the constant shelling. That's where they were hiding when a gang of Arrow Cross found them. The Arrow Cross also found food supplies kept by the Gerbeaud confectionery, which operated out of the same building. They were furious to discover such a large stash of food hidden from them.

They began shouting and threatening the people in the cellar. In panic, one of the men protested his noninvolvement: "I'm Swiss! I'm Swiss!"

In the confusion the Arrow Cross decided he must be lying. He must be Jewish. They must all be Jews.

They emptied the whole cellar and marched everyone off at rifle point toward the Arrow Cross Ministry of Food Supply.

Tom hung up the phone, numb.

They had made it so long. The end of the war was so close he could touch it. Tom couldn't accept that his mother and father might be dead. There was only one place to turn for help. He knew Raoul's secret hiding place. There was nothing to do but go there.

It took the young man two days to make his way through the gunfire and rubble, the chaos and corpses that had once been Pest. When he finally reached the secret vault and gave the pass code, Raoul Wallenberg was glad to see him.

"They took my parents," Tom said. "Two days ago. I don't know where they've taken them."

A cloud passed over Raoul's face. When he spoke, his voice was somber. "I'm sorry, Tom," he said. "It's too late now. There's nothing I can do."

It took Tom six months to find out what had happened. The day after their arrest, his parents and all their neighbors were taken to the Danube. His mother, Berta, and his father, Paul, were shot and thrown into the river. This happened at St. Stephen's Square, only a few feet from where, after the war, the Hungarian people would erect a statue to the honor of Raoul Wallenberg.

Raoul was too restless to stay put in the safety of a bank vault. His maps showed that the Russians were already in control of City Park. He decided to move to the headquarters of the Red Cross on Benczur Street. That way, he'd be among the first to be "liberated" by the Allies when the Soviet army arrived. He was safe on Benczur Street, and the occupants of the Red Cross villa had plenty to eat. But Raoul secretly left each night on missions to take food supplies to the starving people in the ghetto.

With the Soviet army only blocks from the ghetto, surely the SS realized it was too late for its plan of mass murder. But Pal Szalai was the first to get wind of the plan.

A Hungarian officer rushing through the lobby of Town Hall bumped into him. Szalai stopped the man: "Just where are you going in such a hurry?" he asked.

"Five hundred soldiers of the Reich and twenty-two Arrow Cross are on alert at the Royal Hotel. They're requesting two hundred of our Hungarian police to help finish off the ghetto. If we don't get there right away, they're going to start the firing squads without us."

As soon as the officer was out of sight, Szalai found Szabo. "Get to Wallenberg," he said. "Tell him this is it. The pogrom is about to start. Tell him I'm heading straight to Erno Vajna."

Wallenberg met Szalai and together they went to see Vajna. Raoul used all of his best arguments to stop this "monstrous action." He brought to bear every ounce of fortitude he had, as if he could will Vajna to see the truth, to stop the massacre.

But Erno Vajna didn't care anymore. Not about Raoul Wallenberg's outrage, not about the seventy thousand people about to be murdered, not even about saving his own skin. He admitted he knew all about the plan. In fact, he even had his own part to play in it. But stop it? No. Absolutely not.

Minutes were running out. The Hungarian officer and the thin Swede in the long winter coat hurriedly conferred by their cars.

"There's only one person who can stop this," said Wallenberg.

Szalai finished his thought. "General August Schmidthuber."

"We've got to get to him fast."

"Wallenberg, you can't go. The only power we've got over Schmidthuber is you and your determination to hold him responsible. If you march into SS headquarters, he'll have you killed. It's only prudent. Hell, if I were him, I'd have you killed. Go, quickly, where you can't be found. I'll go to Schmidthuber myself with a personal message from Raoul Wallenberg."

Raoul looked thoughtfully at his unlikely ally, the new friend whom he'd judged correctly on that bitter day. "Then let me add to the message," Raoul said. After they talked briefly, Raoul got into his car and disappeared into the streets of Pest.

Szalai went straight to the general's office back at Town

Hall. "General. A message has come in from Raoul Wallenberg. I thought you'd be interested in hearing it."

General Schmidthuber turned and stared at him.

"Wallenberg says that if you don't stop this pogrom, the Swede will personally see to it that you're charged with murder and genocide by the War Crimes Tribunal."

Schmidthuber continued to stare at Szalai. How could this Wallenberg know what was going on, even before it happened? Why could no one find this man?

Well, it was too late to find him now. Unlike Vajna, General Schmidthuber cared very much about saving his own skin. Torn and tired, the general paced up and down the floor of his headquarters. Finally he went to the phone. "Get Lucska from the Arrow Cross, the head of the German garrison, and Vajna, representing Hungary. Here, in my office, right away. *Schnell!*"

Angrily, he smashed the phone back into its cradle.

When the men assembled expectantly, Schmidthuber told them crisply, "There will be no massacre. The pogrom is canceled."

28.

The Mystery Begins

On Saturday, January 13, 1945, Soviet soldiers finally "liberated" the villa on Benczur Street. Twenty Russian soldiers came up through the trapdoor from the cellar.

They asked everyone in the house for their papers. Raoul explained he was a Swedish diplomat who had been running a large operation to save Hungarian Jews. He said he wanted to reach Soviet Marshal Malinovsky as soon as possible. He wanted to make immediate plans to help the more than one hundred thousand people left without food and the necessities of life. Hundreds of children were starving.

The foot soldiers, confused about what to do with him, called their superior, Major Dimitri Demchinkov. Wallenberg and the major talked for more than an hour. If Raoul was a diplomat, the Russian didn't understand why he wasn't with the other diplomats in Buda or why he wanted to meet with Marshal Rodion Malinovsky. Demchinkov decided to continue the conversation at the new Soviet headquarters. Raoul had been hoping for such an invitation. He and Vilmos Langfelder left for the appointment in the blue Studebaker.

The others at the house expected Raoul to come back within hours. They didn't see him again until January 17.

When Wallenberg and Langfelder returned, they had a Russian escort. Raoul explained to his friends that he'd gotten permission to see Marshal Malinovsky at his headquarters in Debrecen, a little more than a hundred miles away.

"Are you crazy?" one of his friends asked. "It's dangerous out there. They're still shooting in Buda."

Raoul said, "It's a little late to change my mind. To tell you the truth, I'm not sure whether I'm their guest or their prisoner."

He gathered his things, including his trusty knapsack, and got the money he'd left there for safekeeping. He bid his friends farewell, then got into the car that Vilmos was driving and roared off with the Soviet guard.

Their next stop was on Tatra Street, where Rezso Muller and his staff were working on their relief plan. Raoul gave Rezso the money he'd just picked up for relief efforts and told him to keep working. He'd be back from Debrecen, ready to shift into high gear, within a week, eight days at the most.

As he stood on the sidewalk talking to Paul Nevi, the manager of the Swedish hospital that he'd set up a few doors down, two old men with yellow stars still stitched to their jackets walked by, free for the first time since March, ten months before.

Raoul smiled. "I'm glad to see my mission wasn't all in vain," he said.

As he turned toward the car, he slipped on the ice and fell. Paul Nevi helped him up.

Raoul climbed into the backseat of the car, as he had

done so many times on so many dangerous missions, and Villy drove off. The war was over. He was finally on a mission of hope.

They sped down the Budapest street with their Russian escorts close behind. Neither Raoul nor Vilmos was ever seen in the free world again.

29.

Raoul Disappears

Somewhere along the road out of Budapest a sinister event took place. Wallenberg's military guard was exchanged for officers from the NKVD, the Soviet secret police now known as the KGB.

Raoul and Vilmos were flown to Moscow, the capital of the Soviet Union. There they were taken to Lubianka Prison and separated from each other.

The Soviet Union and the United States, once allies, mistrusted each other after the war. In Budapest, Raoul's co-workers at the Swedish Legation were harshly questioned by the "liberating" Soviets. "Where did your money come from?" each person was asked. "Were you spying for the Americans, too?"

In February 1945, Raoul's mother, Maj Von Dardel, was told by the Soviet ambassador to Sweden that Raoul was safe in Russia. He warned her not to make a fuss and promised that her son would be back home soon.

But in August, six months later, the story changed completely. In answer to questions about Raoul, Soviet Foreign Minister Andrei Vishinsky replied, "Wallenberg is not in the Soviet Union and is unknown to us." He added it was most likely that Raoul had been killed during street fighting while still in Budapest.

Months passed, then long, frustrating years. A harsh dictator, Josef Stalin, ruled the Soviet Union. As in Nazi-occupied Hungary, thousands of Stalin's citizens simply "disappeared." Many were killed because their beliefs differed from those of the ruling Communist party. Others spent years in a large prison system run by the KGB, sometimes being sent to prison camps, called gulags, located in the vast, snowy wastelands of Siberia.

Nearly a decade after Raoul's incredible work in Budapest, the Soviets started releasing "war criminals" who had completed their jail terms. Some of those men had seen or communicated with Raoul.

The Wallenberg family continued to press the Soviet government for answers. Now the official Soviet answer was that Raoul had been in Lubianka Prison. They claimed he died of a heart attack in 1947 at the young age of thirty-five. But they had no records, no death certificate. More important, they had no body.

Over the next decades, reports of Raoul's whereabouts continued to surface.

Andre Shimkevich, a French student, was interested in Communism. But when he went to Russia in 1929 to study the government, he was arrested as a spy. He had spent eighteen years in gulag prisons, and for two days in December 1947 he shared a cell with Raoul. The two men weren't allowed to speak. But using sign language Raoul told him that he had been accused of spying. This was five months after Raoul's alleged heart attack.

General Gennadi Kuprianov, a Soviet World War II general, himself became a political prisoner. When he was transferred to a gulag far out in Siberia in 1953, he shared a three-week train trip with Raoul. The two men became friends. They met twice again in the prison infirmary in 1955 and 1956. After the general was released and his story reached the West, he was re-arrested and commanded to retract his story. He refused and died suddenly in police custody of a "heart attack."

In January 1961, Dr. Nanna Svartz, a respected Swedish professor and Maj's own doctor, was speaking at a conference in Moscow. One of her oldest friends was Dr. Aleksandr Maiashnikov, a leading Soviet doctor, who told Dr. Svartz that he had examined Raoul Wallenberg personally and that he was being held in a mental hospital in Moscow.

When the Swedish government requested more information, Dr. Maiashnikov changed his story. He'd never heard of Wallenberg, he said. Twice more the Swedish government asked to see the doctor. The second time they were told he wasn't available to answer questions. It seems that he, too, died suddenly of a heart attack.

A Jewish man who ran an opera studio in Moscow was arrested for "economic crimes." He met Raoul in Butyrka Prison in 1974. When the man was freed, he tried to smuggle information about Raoul out of the U.S.S.R. After he finally succeeded, he was re-arrested and hasn't been seen since.

In 1989, the "new" Soviet government invited Raoul's brother and sister (Maj had since died) to Moscow to discuss the case. The Soviet Union returned Raoul's passport and a few personal items. Even when presented with overwhelming firsthand evidence about Raoul's whereabouts, Soviet officials stuck to the story about the 1947 heart attack. They asked if the family wanted to see the grave. No body was there, though, they explained. It was only a headstone.

In August 1991, the new Russian president, Boris Yeltsin, seized all the KGB's secret files. He promised to release the files on Raoul Wallenberg. Such promises have been made several times before by several "new" Soviet leaders. The world is still waiting to learn the truth.

The statue erected to Raoul Wallenberg in Budapest's St. Stephen's Park (Szent Istvan Square). The Communists removed the statue before its official unveiling. Tom Veres took this picture on a Friday. By Sunday, the statue was gone. (Photography by Thomas Veres)

30.

The Making of a Hero

Raoul Wallenberg was, in many ways, an ordinary person. He wasn't a general or a politician or even a diplomat. He was a young man who stood up for his beliefs. By inspiring others to action, he proved that courage is contagious and that one person can truly make a difference.

His family, along with many others, will never stop trying to find out what happened to Raoul Wallenberg, the hero of Budapest. They continue to hope that somehow he must still be alive.

But, perhaps, the best tribute to Raoul Wallenberg comes from the girls and boys, women and men, who hear his story, take it into their hearts, and follow his example.

Index

Make books your companion
Let your bookshelf be your garden—
Judah Ibn Tibbon

to become a member –
to present a gift –

call 1 (800) 234-3151
or write:
The Jewish Publication Society
1930 Chestnut Street
Philadelphia, Pennsylvania 19103

A Jewish Tradition